Leadership of Place

Also available from Bloomsbury

Changing Urban Education, Simon Pratt-Adams, Meg Maguire and Elizabeth Burn

Education and Social Change: Connecting Local and Global Perspectives, edited by Geoffrey Elliott, Chahid Fourali and Sally Issler

Leadership of Place

Stories from Schools in the US, UK and South Africa

KATHRYN RILEY

B L O O M S B U R Y
LONDON • NEW DELHI • NEW YORK • SYDNEY

Bloomsbury Academic

An imprint of Bloomsbury Publishing Plc

50 Bedford Square	175 Fifth Avenue
London	New York
WC1B 3DP	NY 10010
UK	USA

www.bloomsbury.com

First published 2013

British Library Cataloguing-in-Publication Data
A catalogue record for this book is available from the British Library.

ISBN: HB: 978-1-4411-7498-7
PB: 978-1-4411-4911-4
PDF: 978-1-4411-5769-0
ePub: 978-1-4411-8146-6

Library of Congress Cataloging-in-Publication Data
A catalog record for this title is available from the Library of Congress.

Typeset by Deanta Global Publishing Services, Chennai, India
Printed and bound in India

CONTENTS

FOREWORD

The power of place

John MacBeath

Place. It is a simple term with many meanings and profound connotations. We are enjoined from an early age to know our place and 'knowing' our place becomes the work of a lifetime. As a teenager I came to Scotland from another place. I was to be known through my school life as 'Yank', a word strangely new to me as a Canadian, but it put me in my place as someone from somewhere exotic where movies came from – an immigrant with high cachet! My education hitherto, deemed to be inferior due to a lack of Latin, placed me in a class below my own age group in a boy's selective schools with all the male inhibitions, bravado and repression that came with that social, psychological and physical territory. How different might life have been had the accident of place taken a different trajectory.

The bonus was being able to take an outsider's view, an anthropological perspective on what all my classmates took as inevitable, as goldfish for whom water is the milieu and the bowl is the universe. If travel broadens the mind its pay off comes when we return to what we once knew and begin to know it for the first time.

There is place called school. It needs no password to get in, but it is very difficult to get out of. As Kathryn writes, you can learn the password, but the language of the tribe may always elude you. When Bernstein invented the notion of a 'restricted code', accessible to those who understand school's arcane linguistic conventions, it reached much deeper than language to way of seeing the world and the place that school occupies within it. For those who plot a path effortlessly through school, it is hard to understand how the other half lives, struggling to navigate the terrain. How could schools, so familiar and collegial, be construed as dangerous places? But for some young people, the tensions and threats which characterize their neighbourhoods are carried through into classrooms and the spaces between them.

The connect and disconnect between the life of the classroom and the life of the neighbourhood is nowhere better illustrated than in the award-winning film *Entre Les Murs*, set in a Paris multiracial suburb. In its closing scene, the school year is at its end and the classroom teacher sits exhausted behind his desk. As the rest of the class escape to freedom, a teenage girl stays behind to have the last word – 'Sir, I have learned nothing'. It is a poignant end to the film but leaves hanging a vital question. What has she learnt – about authority, relationships, race, sex and gender, about a place called school and her place within it?

In opening the door to a richly constructed intellectual space, Kathryn invites us to adventure beyond many of our own preconceptions to reach *beneath* the surface life of school communities, *beyond* the parameters of the school's containing walls and *within* the beliefs that are such powerful forces for maintaining 'the way we do things round here' or, alternatively seeing the unseen – what the Jewish theologian Abraham Heschel describes as 'insight', – the beginning of perceptions to come rather than the extension of perceptions gone by.

John MacBeath
Emeritus Professor, University of Cambridge

Some thoughts about place in the lives of young people in the United States

Karen Seashore Louis

I loved this book. This book compels us to think very hard about all the ways in which place matters. One of the ways in which Kathryn Riley calls us to reflect about place is that she presents us with a wide variety of ways in which place is experienced by young people and school leaders – all of which emerge from her decade of work with urban principals and students. The different experiences and definitions of place emerge in an evocative and powerful way in the stories that she tells throughout the book.

It is hard not to think about place without responding to the personal and artistic context that Kathryn Riley uses to set the stage for this book. I am also taken with Brian Friel's plays, which create an explicit conflict between where you *live* and where you are *from*. I found myself thinking that neither I nor many of the people I know in the United States have a home place. As a nation populated largely by immigrants and settlers, it is a luxury to stay where you were born. Most of our families came, whether 150 years or 5 years ago, for a wide variety of reasons but usually because of hardship at 'home' or, in the case of involuntary immigrants, forced resettlement. Arrivals were often chaotic, and people tended to settle down where there were jobs, land and a few people who spoke the same language. My family (part of the wave of Scandinavian immigrants in the mid-to-late 1900s) landed initially in Ohio and Minnesota, but quickly scattered throughout the Midwest. By the time my father's generation had settled down, I had first and second cousins whose names I knew, but who I saw rarely if at all, in California, Illinois, Iowa, Minnesota, New York and Oregon, among others. I grew up in Michigan – but it is hard to say that it was a home place: It was where my nuclear family ended up. I have no family there now.

I was also an observer of the grand experiment of northern US school desegregation in the 1960s and 70s, where social science led to court decisions that required that children be bussed out of their residential neighbourhoods to attend schools that had a mixture of white and black, poor and middle class. The data showed (and continue to suggest) that attending a school that is socio-economically and racially mixed results in higher achievement for the less advantaged student, while not diminishing the opportunities and learning of those who come from more advantaged families. The results of 'forced bussing' were, in many ways, socially positive, but the ideal of a community- or place-based school was lost in American cities.

But we also know from Professor Riley's book that place – meaning the characteristics of the community in which a young person grows up – continues to be a very important determinant of their educational success, irrespective of their talent, their family commitment or the dedication of their teachers to the community. Sociological studies in the United States have established beyond doubt that the resources that are available in the community, along with indicators of neighbourhood distress, have a particularly strong effect on adolescents. Even when they come from resilient families with means to ensure that they thrive, lack of stability in the community is a problem that they take with them into school.

Fast-forwarding from 1960s' desegregation bussing to today, Professor Riley encountered one of the logical outcomes in New York, where families get to choose a school and new schools are viewed as a strategy for increasing academic success. We can see some of the consequences of the loss of a community school, which includes not only loss of place but also resegregation. Recent immigrant and minority families are choosing new charter schools, presumably because they see them as responsive to a different kind of community: a community of identity. In my own city, the yellow school buses are rolling again, but this time to assure families that their children have teachers who look like them, understand their culture and are passionately committed to involving the *community of immigrants with which they identify*. Place is important – but the meaning of place and space has shifted from physical to social.

These are only a few of the reflections that I experienced while reading this wonderful book. Other readers will find their own; all will be enriched by the words that Riley has captured and how she has placed them in the context of our larger aspiration to create schools that can be successful for our most vulnerable students.

Karen Seashore Louis is Regents Professor and Robert H. Beck Chair in the College of Education and Human Development at the University of Minnesota. She has written extensively about school change and urban education.

ACKNOWLEDGEMENTS

I would like to thank all of the schools, their leaders and the young people who are a part of this book for their welcome and for their contributions to my understanding of their lives and experiences. Keith and Catherine Borien of the BEFSA Foundation facilitated my visit to South Africa and Joseph O'Brien and the New York Board of Education facilitated my visit to New York. Many thanks indeed to all of them.

A number of people have contributed to my understanding of the issues presented in this book. They include colleagues from the Institute of Education who worked with me on the project 'Leadership on the Front-line' or were part of the London Education Research Unit team, as well as many of my students over the years.

Particular thanks to friends and colleagues who have commented on the evolution of this book – Tanya Arroba, Anita Berlin, Gerald Grace, Diane Hofkins, Bob Hope, Trisha Jaffe, Karen Seashore Louis, Vanessa Ogden, Dinesh Ramjee, Louise Stoll and Rob Thomas.

A NOTE ON THE AUTHOR

Kathryn was born in Manchester. After voluntary service at the Asmara Teacher Institute Eritrea, she taught in inner-city schools in London. She has held political office in London as a directly elected member of the Inner London Education Authority and has also been a local authority Chief Officer.

Kathryn was first appointed as a Professor in 1993. She is currently Director of Research at the London Centre for Leadership in Learning, Institute of Education.

Kathryn's international research has taken her to many countries. She has worked with a number of international agencies, including the World Bank, where she headed the Effective Schools and Teachers Group. She is particularly interested in how change takes place in the field of education and the contribution of school leaders, staff, students and communities to the process of change.

PREFACE

The notion of place is a powerful one: the place where we are from; the place where we live; the place we would like to be. It signifies issues about identity and belonging (or lack of it) and about roots and connections (or lack of them). Place provides poets, playwrights, musicians, artists, etc. with rich harvests to reap.

In a fluid, uncertain world, place matters. Place is a physical entity, a building, a location that is important to us. It's also an emotional response to the world around us: connected to our sense of self, identity, worth. This book is about the importance of place in the lives of young people. It explores the ways in which school leaders can help young people find their place in the world.

The book offers 'stories', vignettes which give a sense of the complexities of young people's lives. These are drawn from nearly 100 schools and the lives and experiences of 300 school leaders and 700 young people in those schools. The schools are in socially disadvantaged urban communities in the United States and the United Kingdom and impoverished rural communities in South Africa. The young people whose lives appear in the pages of this book are at the cutting-edge of shaping and reshaping what it means to live in a multicultural society. How they deal with this and how they find their place in the world is the business of school.

Leadership of place has many levels within a school. It is about responding to the challenges and contradictions in young people's lives. School can be a place of welcome and belonging. It can provide spaces where young people feel secure, free to speak out: spaces which encourage them to be creative and develop their autonomy. School can also be a place of rejection and exclusion: the spaces within it hostile and unsafe. If young people are to reach for the stars, take their role as global citizens and pass on their learning to future generations, they first need to have a sense of place and belonging and be secure in the belief who they are. The notion of leadership of place which is at the heart of the book is about making this possible.

Introduction

Place divided

Finding a place

Kushtrim[1] had moved to England to avoid ethnic conflict at home in Albania. During his first year in school he was quiet and withdrawn. His schoolmates kept their distance from him. The hardship and suffering etched on his face made him look older and tougher than he was. His London teacher told me:

> In Year 2011, his English improved significantly, allowing him to become loud, outspoken and even verbally aggressive, which made him popular with students but feared and disliked by teachers. Incidents with teachers were numerous and threatening with physical violence became Kushtrim's trade mark. He challenged almost every school rule, especially the ones that he felt were 'institutionalising' and subjugating him, such as the school uniform and classroom etiquette rules.
>
> He wore an Albanian flag and a metal two-headed eagle around his neck and regularly refused to take them off. It was all he had left from his country, the only familiar thing. . . .
>
> (Stabler 2011)

Kushtrim's story – more of which later – is a telling reminder of the importance of place (sometimes mental, often physical) for one young person as he struggles to find his identity in an alien culture.

This book is a series of stories of people and of places. The stories are connected by the insights they provide about our understanding of place. They are told from the perspectives of young people in a range of cultures and contexts as well as from those who lead the schools they attend.

The exploration of the notion of place which is at the heart of this book is not an abstract pursuit, an academic exercise which lies outside the realms of daily reality. It is inextricably linked to the lives and experiences of the young people in our schools as they seek to find a place for themselves in our world. Ongoing population movements mean that young people inhabit a world of increasing diversity and complexity. This is a world that some people fear. The communities in which young people live can be divided: young people caught up in experiences that would tax the most resilient adult. And yet this changing world offers opportunities for new learning, new understanding.

The power of place resonates in many ways. Animals mark their terrain. Gangs assert their territory. It is a physical reality and an emotional response. In a world of social transformation – your place matters. Place takes on a range of meanings for those who have been unwilling exiles, part of the world's diasporas (be they Irish, Jewish or Somalian), forced to leave their homes by economic, political or social factors beyond their control.

In this book, I explore the notion of place and the implications of this concept for schools and their leaders. My argument is that all young people, and particularly those in our most challenging and disadvantaged communities, need to be secure in their beliefs about who they are, where they are from, where they now find themselves and where they want to be.

This sense of identity is important if they are to find their place in the world and become happy and fulfilled individuals.

Finding a space

Place is closely linked to space. Our cities can be 'scary' places for children and young people. There can be spaces that are 'no-go areas' and also places of divisions; for example, 'Newham is a very dangerous borough', one child wrote (see Illustration 0.1).

In Illustration 0.2, provides us vignettes of city life – organized street crime, people too scared to help, etc. To survive, you need to lock up your bike and be safe. Two vignettes stand out: friends and multicultural city life (drawn in different and vibrant colours).

ILLUSTRATION 0.1

ILLUSTRATION 0.2

However, the boundaries and divisions about space and territory are not immovable. 'No-go' zones can be breached. Spaces that were previously alien to young people can become 'cool'. As people begin to shape and reshape those spaces, feel safe and take control, those spaces can become transformed into 'places'. New spaces can be created which will change experiences. This is happening in many different ways around the globe with social movements that aim to transform spaces. City Repair – which began in Portland, Oregon – aims to reclaim urban spaces in order to create more community-oriented public gathering spaces where communities can come together to share their stories, their songs and their lives (Nastasi and Porath 2010).

Enlarging space into place is about interactions, communications and relationships. It is about social capital and it is about doing things differently – which is where leadership of place comes in. The notion of leadership of place stems from an appreciation of the ways in which leaders can enable, support and enact for staff, students and the community. They can support positive interactions, meaningful communication and relationships based on mutuality. Leaders can also block, oppose and fail to achieve. My focus is on the power of what might be: the potential of leaders to tap into the needs of young people, to help them find their place and anchor themselves in this fragile and fluid world.

Leadership of place starts from the outside – the community, the neighbourhood – and is rooted in a sense of partnership. This outside-in construction is distinctively different from the more conventional inside-out approaches to leadership which start with internal workings of the school's community. The internal life of the school is obviously critical: but what this life is, how it operates, needs to be connected to external realities and possibilities. Although the fieldwork for this book has largely focused on those who have formal leadership within a school, are at its helm setting its direction, leaders of place are not only senior leaders. They are also drawn from middle leaders, subject leaders, classroom leaders and young people. For senior leaders, leadership of place is about widening the leadership network.

Leadership of place goes beyond understanding context. It begins with the lives and experiences of young people. Being a

'Leader of Place' is not an attempt to find an excuse for failure: a way of blaming challenging circumstances for underachievement. It is a proactive approach to leadership which recognizes the ways in which leaders can work with others – to cross boundaries, to influence and shape communities and to unleash potential.

Looking through the place lens

Using the place lens to look at the lives of young people offers us a fresh perspective on identity and belonging. It shows the role schools can play in social transformation. The place 'lens' focuses on the importance of developing physical and social conditions within a school that take into account the socio-economic and environmental limitations of a locality, as well as the aspirations of its communities. Educators, be they policy-makers, practitioners, system or school leaders, need to know and understand more about the physical characteristics of a locality, such as its housing and transport; the socio-economic features (e.g. levels of unemployment, social mix); the racial, cultural and ethnic make-up of the community and the relationships between different groups; patterns of mobility and transformation.

These historical and contemporary factors influence the social context and the expectations and beliefs that children and their families bring to their education experience. The notion of place helps us think about what has changed (the historical context); what is still changing; and what is likely to change. It is a reminder of transience, transition and transformation. And it is also a reminder of feelings and emotions, identity and belonging.

In exploring the power of place, my aim in this book is to deepen knowledge and understanding about the role of schools and their leaders in our uncertain times. I want to encourage a re-appraisal of the importance of place in our thinking about schools. I offer examples of the kinds of 'leaderly' actions, associated with leadership of place, which are needed to build trust and collaboration between schools and communities. I hope that this book will be helpful to practitioners, policy makers and researchers, adding to understanding about the ways in which identity and belonging, inclusion and exclusion are woven together.

Divided communities

When I leave this meeting with you, I will go home and not see another white face until I come back here next week.

(Young Muslim, Pakistani man, living in Lancashire)

I never met anyone on this estate who wasn't like us from around here.

(Young white man, living in Lancashire)

Class, gender, ethnicity, faith and generation all shape the ways in which individuals and groups experience place, respond to place and identify with place. The enormous geographical mobility and displacement that characterizes our modern global world reinforces the importance of the new found place and deepens the profound attachment that individuals and communities have to their place. Understanding more about these issues will enable schools to respond to the needs of young people, in ways that can help transform lives: their lives and ours.

One significant aspect of place for many young people from disadvantaged areas is the degree to which their daily lives are shaped by the experience of living in divided communities. Take, for example, some of the towns in the North of England: Bradford, Leeds, Burnley and Oldham. In 2001, community divisions led to confrontations between white and Asian youths and ultimately erupted into a series of race riots. One finding from the Cantle Commission of Inquiry, set up in the wake of the riots, was the extent to which white and Asian youths lived separate and distinctively different lives. The two quotations which begin this section are both taken from evidence given to the Commission (Cantle 2001).

This book explores young people's experience of life in divided communities.

● Divisions can be *physical*, as in the example from the Cantle Inquiry where communities of residence are permanent and demarked. These demarcations are embedded in political and historical circumstances. Other examples I will draw on of this physical divide include Northern Ireland, where sectarian divisions remain entrenched, and South Africa where the historical divisions of Apartheid serve to maintain a relatively racially segregated housing and schooling system.

- Divisions can be *socio-economic*, effecting where families live, as well as where young people go to school. Those factors influence whether young people attend school in relatively affluent, or in disadvantaged areas: whether they attend privately funded, or state funded schools. Socioeconomic divisions, as well as Apartheid, are another part of South Africa's contemporary story. The locality study on Brooklyn New York highlights the ways in which young people from poorer communities, many of whom are from Afro-American or Hispanic backgrounds, can find themselves attending school in localities which are predominately white and relatively wealthy: in a community but not of it.

- Divisions can be *imported* by refugees from their own history, as is partly the case in Kustrim's story. Refugees from both sides of a conflict in war-torn countries, such as Somalia, may find themselves in their newly adopted countries living and attending school in close proximity to each other. The young people may feel pressurized to continue old divisions: perpetuating some of the battles of their parents.

- Divisions may also be a product of *immigration* and rapid shifts in population, as the illustration from London's Isle of Dogs suggests later in the book. In recent decades, the Isle of Dogs has been an area of rapid changes. Housing policies have resulted in growing numbers of Bangladeshis in what was a predominantly white working-class community. Discontent has been the fodder for extremist groups and has led to clashes between the latest arrivals and the more established white and Afro-Caribbean communities.

- Divisions may also be created by *gangs*. The prevalence of gangs and their impact on the lives of young people is a common feature of life for many young people in this book. While a decade ago the clashes in the Isle of Dogs were between newly arrived and established communities, contemporary sources of conflict are more likely to be gang-related and within communities, for example, between different groups of Bangladeshi males.

Divisions create insiders and outsiders. Those who feel safe and those who don't. Divisions restrict young people's views and perceptions of what is possible.

Differences can manifest themselves in different ways: overtly 'you look different to me', or could be put more subtly. The question 'where are you from?' may appear innocuous. However, the answer can be fraught with meaning, signifying differences in tribe, faith or political allegiance. The question 'Where are you from?' asked in Northern Ireland could elicit two very different responses:

● 'I'm from Derry'.

● 'I'm from Londonderry'.

Derry/Londonderry still remains a divided city. The answer 'Derry' to the question 'Where are you from?' is preferred by predominantly Catholic nationalists, and the answer 'Londonderry' by mainly Protestant Unionists. While giving the answer today may not be as dangerous as it was in the past but the response still holds meaning.

When asked the question 'Where are you from?' I usually answer along the following lines:

● I'm from Manchester but I live in London.

If the conversation continues, I might indicate my origins (I'm a Celt with some Lithuanian Jewish infusions) and go on to talk about my tribe (Lancashire Irish) and describe behaviours characteristic of that tribe: Labour voting, supporters of Manchester United, Catholic. Prompted further, I might add that I was born in Wythenshawe, then a white working-class estate. It was one of the largest social housing developments in the United Kingdom built as part of post-World War II regeneration of Manchester. In the aftermath of the War, the move to Wythenshawe for my family, as for many others, symbolized a new beginning, away from bomb-damaged areas and the constraints and limitations of inner-city life. Knowing where I am from, and where my ancestors had their roots, is part of my identity. It helps me locate myself today in my adopted city of London and my place in the world.

Different places in the world

At the heart of the book are three locality studies which serve to illuminate the educational challenges facing schools and colleges serving our most needy communities. Two focus on highly disadvantaged urban communities, one in the United States (Brooklyn, New York), the other in Britain (London's East End), with the third looking at impoverished rural communities in South Africa (the Eastern Cape). The contrasts and similarities which emerge from the three locality studies help us understand the importance of place in shaping meaning and identity. They also serve to demonstrate the relevance and complexity of the concept for schools, educators and policy makers.

Throughout the book I have offered many examples of the significance of place. These are more than isolated vignettes of good practice and are used to illustrate a broader perspective on change which asks:

- *What* can be done?
- *Who* can make a difference?
- *When?*
- *Where?*
- *How?*

This framework is based on what we know from empirical research in a number of fields, leadership and management, school improvement and student inclusion, knowledge of best practice. It is also shaped by my own childhood in Manchester and by my experiences as a teacher and – for several years – as a London politician with responsibility for education.

Broadly speaking, it is a theory of action. I offer this as a scaffold for analysing the issues and for shaping a response. It is not a one size fits all prescription which all schools and education institutions should follow regardless. It is a framework for a change process which, if it is to be successful, requires the collaboration of the many partners who have both a direct and indirect interest in those institutions. These include staff, parents, pupils, local community members and policy-makers. Implicit within the framework is a view that the process of transforming our challenging schools is messy and complicated.

For me, key elements of the framework derive from a belief in boundless possibilities for, and with, the children and young people in our impoverished areas. Implicit in the theory of action is a wish to reach out beyond the narrow stereotypes of what our children and young people can achieve and can be. It is also about helping to create a new vision of learning which draws them towards the cultural and historical riches and opportunities that are available to them, although often masked.

Too often our children are labelled and categorized in ways that are unhelpful and limiting. Assumptions are made about their postcode (affluent or poor), their immigration status (refugee or immigrant), their family circumstances (stable or chaotic). There are many dismissive attitudes about social housing estates, such as Wythenshawe. Sweeping negative generalizations can dismiss whole communities. Estates such as Wythenshawe are no longer the homogeneous communities they were in my day. There are problems on many of these estates today, including poverty, gangs, unemployment and drugs, and there are many parents who find it difficult to cope with the day-to-day challenges of city or estate living. Some are suspicious of authority, antagonistic or uncooperative towards school. However, in my experience, there are few parents who do not want the best for their children. They may be anti-school, or anti-authority but they are rarely anti-education.[2] Through understanding more about the lives and experiences of families and communities, and of the young people within those communities, schools and colleges can help alter the dynamics of those relationships.

Questions for Discussion and Reflection

1 Do the young people you work with experience their life as divided? If so, what are the divisions?

2 What's your answer to the question: 'Where are you from?'

3 What did you find out about yourself from answering that question?

The book has seven main chapters.

Chapter 1:

Place for me? Explores the importance of place in our psyche, why we yearn for home, why we scramble for a space to be ourselves and why we want to turn that space into our place. The notion of place as a foundation stone for social meaning and social interaction is powerful.

Finding a place that is ours can be difficult, particularly if we come as recent immigrants motivated by a desire to improve our lot in life, or driven by fears of wars and or mayhem. Disputes between newly arrived and long standing communities for place have led to political interventions to reduce conflict and promote cohesion. As governments have sought to promote cohesion or reshape how communities live alongside each other, schools have been drawn into this policy arena.

Chapter 2:

A place in the city? Investigates the patterns that shape the lives of city dwellers today. It examines the particular struggles that the poor and displaced face in making and maintaining a place for themselves in the city. To illustrate these issues, the chapter throws a spotlight on London, highlighting how it has changed over recent decades and examining the implications of these changes for young people, and for schools and their leaders.

Chapter 3:

Is this place always changing? Draws on *Leadership on the Front-line, a* project which involved some 70 headteachers and school principals in the UK, to examine some of the complexities of context and place. This exploration is made through the eyes of school leaders in London, Liverpool, Birmingham, Cardiff, Manchester and Belfast as well as through those of young people. I make the argument that school leaders can create the space for the voices of marginalized and disenfranchised to be heard. By working in partnerships with staff, pupils and communities, schools can become not only safe spaces but also places of opportunity: something very precious in a crowded world.

Chapter 4:

What's in a neighbourhood? – *Stories from Brooklyn, New York* is the first of the three detailed locality studies. The perspectives on place in this chapter are from the standpoints of school principals and students. The stories they tell give a sense of the complexities of young people's lives and the challenges they face. While the neighbourhood school still exists in New York, growing numbers of young people travel from their 'hoods', to neighbourhoods which are very different from the daily worlds they habit. For them, the notion and experience of place has its own complexities.

Chapter 5:

What's in this global city for me? – *Stories from London's East End* delves into the contrasting worlds of the East End. The East End encapsulates the versatility of London as a diverse global city of opportunities, challenges and contradictions. For many young people the contrasts between street-life and school-life are significant, as they struggle to find a place for themselves in a world that can be alien.

Chapter 6:

What's my location? – *Stories from the Eastern Cape, South Africa* is enriched by vivid drawings and illustrations from the young people. The locality focus is the municipality of Nkonkobe, a particularly impoverished rural area in the Eastern Cape. Unemployment is 80 per cent. There is limited infrastructure and many adults seek employment in the major cities while young people and the elderly remain in the locations. Schools play a central role in the lives of young people.

Chapter 7:

A place in this world distils some of the lessons learnt from the three locality studies and the vignettes. It develops the theory of action outlined earlier in this chapter and draws on two conceptual filters – political literacy and social trust – to take this further.

It offers a framework for *seeing* things differently and *doing* things differently and for considering the implications of place for policy and practice, as well as for global citizenship. For to be able to think and contribute as a global citizen, young people first need to become secure in *who* they are. Having a sense of place and location – and a view that they can influence their own lives – will free them to take up their role as citizens and as fulfilled human beings.

Questions:

The end of each chapter offers the reader a series of questions. These are for individual reflection and for discussion with others. The questions encourage thinking about the personal implications of place as well as the implications for educators and young people.

Notes

1 Pseudonyms have been used for the names of students, staff and schools.

2 I have written elsewhere about my own time as a teacher in challenging inner city schools, in the 1970s and 1980s and the ways in which that experience influenced my thinking and my practice (Riley 2008).

CHAPTER ONE

Place for me?

My home, my place

Few authors have captured the importance of place in our psyche as successfully as Irish playwright Brian Friel has done. Friel's work illustrates the centrality of place for people of diasporas, who leave their homelands for new opportunities, and for communities who seek redress for past injuries. Thoughts of place and home can trigger feelings of deep longing as well as a sense of belonging and hope. In Friel's play *Dancing at Lughnasa*, Michael looks back to the summer of his youth in which his mother and her sisters danced with abandon and joy.

When I cast my mind back to that summer of 1936, different kinds of memories offer themselves to me. We got our first wireless set that summer – well, a sort of a set; and it obsessed us. And because it arrived as August was about to begin, my Aunt Maggie – she was the joker of the family – she suggested we give it a name. She wanted to call it Lugh after the old Celtic God of the Harvest. Because in the old days August the First was La Lughnasa, the feast day of the pagan god, Lugh; and the days and weeks of harvesting that followed were called the Festival of Lughnasa. But Aunt Kate – she was a national schoolteacher and a very proper woman – she said it would be sinful to christen an inanimate object with any kind of name, not to talk of a pagan god. So we just called it Marconi because that was the name emblazoned on the set.

. . . I remember my first delight, indeed my awe, at the sheer magic of that radio. . . . I remember the kitchen throbbing with the beat of Irish dance music beamed to us all the way from Dublin, and my mother and her sisters suddenly catching hands and dancing a spontaneous step-dance and laughing – screaming! – like excited schoolgirls.

Friel was born in Omagh, County Tyrone (Boltwood 2007). In *Dancing at Lughnasa*, Friel captures the poignancy of a community whose hopes and dreams are slowly eroded, as social and economic forces push the community gradually, inexorably, into decline. The only way out is to leave Ireland. By the end of the play, Michael's family has become divided: two of the sisters have departed to London, never to be seen again. Michael has witnessed the last occasion on which the four sisters would dance together.

In *The Home Place*, Friel grapples with the notion of identity. The context for the play is the resurgence of the Home Rule for Ireland movement in the summer of 1878. Landowner Christopher Gore, a main character in the play, has to answer the question: *Whose side are you on?* The choice for Gore is between the country of his birth (England) and the country in which he now owns land and property (Ireland). For many immigrants and refugees today, the question *Whose side are you on?* Can be a difficult one, particularly when there is conflict. It forces them to reconcile feelings about the land of their birth with those of their adopted homes.

'Home' is a fragile concept, idealized by those who have become part of the world's diasporas. I live in London but remain a Mancunian. Yet, connections to birthplace and home ties have loosened in many Western contemporary societies. Change of residences has become more common. People move around their neighbourhood, their towns, their cities, within countries or to different countries. And yet, the place where we are from is essential to our identity and to the stories we tell of our lives.

In *The Freedom of the City*, Friel tackles issues of place, power and belonging. The play is set in Derry, Northern Ireland, in 1973, in the aftermath of the Roman Catholic Civil Rights meeting which, following the death of 13 protestors, came to be known as Bloody Sunday. It centres on three protesters who accidentally find themselves in the mayor's parlour in the Guildhall: an action that is interpreted as an 'occupation' and which leads to their deaths. People can find themselves in the wrong place at the wrong time.

Space and place

The scramble for space

The struggle for place begins first with a struggle for space. Mamphela Ramphele captures this battle for space in her powerful book on the lives of the migrant labour hostel dwellers of Cape Town, South Africa. Its evocative title, 'A Bed Called Home', reminds us of the power of the concepts of space and place. The hostel dwellers in a spartan and crowded building in South Africa have taken their only personal space (their bed) and turned that space into their home: an act that expresses the need we all have to find some space with which to identify. Ramphele (1993) charts the many dimensions of space, arguing that the capacity of the hostel dwellers to act is constrained by their limited access to political, social, economic, intellectual and psychological space. In this analysis of the multidimensional nature of space, Ramphele suggests that the space individuals inhabit has a profound impact on their sense of self.

> To a large extent inhabited space has a major impact on the self-image of individuals and their perception of their place in society. For hostel dwellers, interesting questions arise about the impact of the constant assault on their dignity in the work environment, where they do menial jobs, and in their accommodation, with its squalor and lack of privacy.
>
> (Ramphele 1993, p. 7)

Inhabited space shapes expectations and aspirations, and views about place in society. Political decisions shape access to *physical space* – in terms of both quality and quantity. Ramphele demonstrates the ways in which the many different aspects of space have a profound effect on individuals, in terms of intellectual expectations, as well as their assumptions about the norms of behaviour and relationships. Reflecting on the experiences of the labour hostel dwellers, she concludes that the 'inhabitated space' that individuals find themselves in provides them with cues that encourage them to expand or contract their expectations.

Notions of space can be translated into the world of the school and the world that young people inhabit around their school. In an interesting book on young people in our global cities, Jo-Anne Dillabough and Jacqueline Kennelly (2010) put forward three concepts to help us think about space and locality for young people. I have provided examples of young people's drawings from the project *Leadership on the Front*-line (which is discussed more fully in Chapter 3) which seem to exemplify each of the concepts. The young people interviewed as part of the project were asked to depict their daily lives, illustrating the good and bad features.

- The first of these concepts of space for young people is the notion of *particular spaces*, such as the corridors within a school, as fluid arenas in which relationships are constantly being reshaped. The school corridor is often an area within the school that is free from teacher-based authority. In this vacuum, relationships between students can emerge in powerful ways, both positively or negatively – through, for example, bullying or racism.

In Illustration 1.1, a student from an inner-city school in London has drawn the corridor space. It is a lonely and empty area that suddenly can become a packed, bustling thoroughfare. The arrows indicate which direction to walk, and the identical doors presage the moment when unknown groups of students will pour out of them into the corridor.

- The second concept of space refers to *particular localities* and to the knowledge that shapes young people's views about who they are in relation to those localities. The everyday activities, experiences and cultural practices in their neighbourhood influence how young people see themselves as being valued in the wider world. I have included many examples of this in the three locality studies later in the book. To illustrate the point here I have included Illustration 1.2 a drawing made by a young child from Manchester. It depicts his sadness about some of the experiences he encounters in his local area. What he faces

ILLUSTRATION 1.1

ILLUSTRATION 1.2

on the street is very different from what he experiences at school. His text reads:

> I heyt gun shots. (I hate gun shots.)
>   I heyt wen the sun gets in my ice. (I hate it when the sun gets in my eyes.)

- The third concept is to do with space and *new and emerging forms of social conflict*. It picks up on the resentment that some young people experience when they are caught up in events in which they have little or no control, or when they are blamed for the actions of others. Dissent can manifest itself in a number of ways, such as particular forms of popular culture, such as rap. In illustration 1.3, which is from Derry/Londonderry, the resentment is palpable. The 'louts' get all the attention. Part of the text in the illustration reads:

> Louts/hoods are recognised more than the good children . . . We're treated the same as the hoods! Looked down upon . . .

ILLUSTRATION 1.3

As the three images demonstrate, young people can struggle to come to terms with the space around them. The space may be alien, unsafe, threatening. The space they inhabit in their locality may not feel like their place because it is a place divided.

The struggle for place

The struggle for place can be ongoing and relentless. In the introduction, I gave the Derry/Londonderry example to illustrate the significance of the question *Where are you from?* and the answer to that question. In the illustration 1.4, again from the project *Leadership on the Frontline*, Mairi illustrates the contrasts in her life in 'L'Derry': a good school and plenty of activities and entertainment but two sides battling against each. The illustration captures her experience

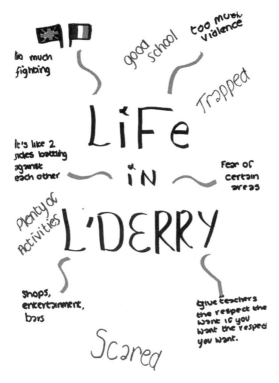

ILLUSTRATION 1.4

of the dividing line which still characterizes the daily encounters and experiences of many. In her experience, it is a place divided. Some people live in fear. She feels trapped and she is scared.

One of the school principals from Northern Ireland involved in Leadership on the Front-line commented on its implications for young people. He voiced his heart-felt concerns for young people on both sides of the sectarian divide thus:

> Our schools are on either side of the community divide but the problems are the same. The kids are fearful, the lawlessness of the town, certain areas they don't feel safe – these are the issues that are coming out for us. Dealing with that is the brutal truth, and to do something constructive about that. I'm quite at a loss to think about it.

While young people in Northern Ireland may have a clear sense of their identity, in terms of their roots, their beliefs their families' political allegiances, in a divided country, the notion of place is fractured and limiting. Place is a foundation stone for social meaning and social interactions. It connects with many stories and many lives. The history of place echoes through the years. In the play *Translations*, Brian Friel highlights the ways in which linguistic, cultural and generational factors influence our experience of place. The play is set in a quiet community in the Ireland of 1833 – just before the potato famine. It is performed in Gaelic and English and charts the progress of an English military expedition whose task it is to map the country[1] and convert all Gaelic place names into English. The star-crossed lovers are an Irish woman who speaks no English and an English soldier who speaks no Irish. Although the villagers have little experience of the outside world, tales of Greek goddesses are commonplace, and Latin and Greek spoken.

The play has become one of the most widely translated and produced plays of the post-World War II era, testimony to the significance of place and identity in our fast moving global world (Wikipedia 2012). The play's power lies in its capacity to communicate the importance for all of finding a home and people to share our lives with.

In *Translations*, the voices of the outsider are heard in different guises. The fragile sense of belonging hangs in the balance. The outsider has to learn life afresh. The outsider may be the person who finds that their homeland is no longer theirs, as is the case for this Irish character in *Translations* who says:

> We must learn those new names . . . We must learn where we live.
> We must learn to make them our own.

The outsider may be the person who seeks to settle in a new country but fears they will never quite belong. These fears are echoed in the words of the English soldier in *Translations* who dreams of the possibility and impossibility of a life in Ireland:

> Even if I did speak Irish I would always be an outsider here, wouldn't I?
> I may learn the password but the language of the tribe will always elude me.

The struggle for place is the struggle not to be an outsider. For the immigrant or refugee who is the outsider, knowing the language, the clues, the codes, of the dominant 'tribe' can be an elusive goal. For the person who becomes an outsider in their own country, the struggle is for physical *space* as well as for the emotional space that shapes relationships (Bourdieu 1999). Place assumes a particular intensity in diverse multicultural, multilingual, multifaith and highly disadvantaged urban communities, where language, culture, mobility and experience can create uncertainties, as well as differing expectations about location and identity (Putnam 2007).[2]

New York's Lower East Side has long been a place in which communities new to the United States have sought to establish roots. In *Place: A Short Introduction* Tim Cresswell charts the history of the Lower East Side over many decades, describing the ways in which it has been home to a succession of immigrant communities: Irish, Jews, Italians, Eastern Europeans, Haitians, Germans and Puerto Ricans. Its sense of social history is heightened as a place of political uprisings and police riots (Cresswell 2004).

Cresswell's story of the Lower East Side shows how important it is for people to have a fixed place that they can point to – *Here is my place . . . Here is your place* – as they seek to find a new identity for themselves as Americans. He illustrates the ways in which those different immigrant communities have sought to recreate their space on the Lower East Side and to link it to their homelands. He writes about tenement walls painted in the rich Caribbean colours of coral, turquoise and yellow which evoke memories of home, and about a Puerto Rican community centre in a garden, built as a 'casita' by Puerto Ricans, and decorated with their national flag.

Cresswell also identifies the contemporary tensions on the Lower East Side: between the wealthy, seeking to colonize a neighbourhood with unexploited real estate opportunities, and the poorer communities seeking to retain their hard-won territory. However, as he points out, the Lower East Side's contemporary story is far from unique. It is:

> Simply an example of what is going on in all human life – a struggle over the very basis of human experience – the need for place as a bedrock of human meaning and social relations.
>
> (Cresswell 2004, p. 32)

Reluctantly in this place

A further complexity in the struggle for place is the degree to which immigrants are driven to seek a new home by positive sentiments, or their need to escape dire situations in their home lands. For some, it can be a mixture of both. Nigerian born, US-based academic John Ogbu coined the terms 'voluntary' and 'involuntary' minorities to capture the experiences of Afro-Americans who had been forcibly brought to the United States as slaves. This coercion, he argued, led to the development of a culture, a sense of social or collective identity resistant to the imposed educational norms and values of the dominant society: a society to which they had been subordinated (Ogbu 1992; Ogbu and Simons 1998). Ogbu went on to argue that 'involuntary' minorities tended to adopt 'oppositional' identities to the mainstream culture. This was in response to a perceived glass ceiling imposed by white society on the job prospects of their parents, and others in their communities.

This analysis throws light on contemporary issues in all three of the locality studies in this book: South Africa, London and New York. The Eastern Cape, the former 'Homelands' of the Ciskei and Transkei, represents the lands where Xhosa-speaking South Africans were forced to move. Both London and New York are receiving centres for international migration. Education is one of the services most challenged by migration. Many young people and their families are seeking new opportunities. Some have bitter regrets at being forced by political and economic circumstances to leave their home. Obgu's analysis helps us understand the experiences and expectations of young people who came with their families to major cities as involuntary immigrants: forced to leave their homes due to famine, war and other related social upheavals.

However, arrival in a new country as a young person with the label refugee or immigrant is only the first part of the process. There is no guarantee that the receiving school is ready to meet the young person's needs (Mehmedbegovic 2007). While most schools set out to do this with a good heart, good faith and good intent, assumptions, misassumptions, long-held beliefs and practices can get in the way. There are further complexities. Refugees and immigrant bring with them very different experiences. The immigrant typically arrives with hopes and aspirations of permanence. For the refugee there is ambivalence. Brought to an alien environment by civil war or famine s/he may have no plan to remain. As an unwilling migrant from their homeland, the response to their new place may be challenging to schools. Divergent world views and misunderstandings add to the complexities of the situation.

Take as an example young people who arrive in many cities across the globe from Somalia, a country which has experienced two decade of war. The emerging literature indicates a pattern of underachievement and alienation from the mainstream culture (Kahin 1997); cultural contradictions and issues related to literacy (Rasmussen 2009). For the young people from Somalia, the values and practices of their home-lives (influenced by their culture and beliefs of the Somalian community as Sunni Muslims) may be at variance with those of their school life which are generally shaped by Christian and secular traditions as well as by the broadly egalitarian customs of wider society. This creates significant leadership challenges in schools. It raises important questions for schools leaders such as:

- *What can they do to understand the cultural frames of reference that create oppositional attitudes?*

- *How can they create a bridge between mainstream and minority cultures?*

- *What do schools need to* jettison from the past and what do they need to keep?
- *What do communities need to* jettison from the past and what do they need to keep?

If these questions are not explored, then the layers of misunderstanding gradually become set in stone. Returning once again to Kushtrim, his story unfolded in the following way.[3] Kushtrim's behaviour became a growing cause for concern in the school. He was being met by increasing impatience on the part of senior staff:

> The choir of the displeased with Kushtrim was reaching its crescendo and he was reciprocating this by threatening staff even more and regularly truanting his ICT lessons.

The school's focus on his bad behaviour had, in her view, taken attention away from the academic gains he had made:

> Nobody noticed . . . that, despite his verbal violence, Kushtrim had never laid his little finger on anybody in the school. Nobody praised him for mastering English in two years so that he could joke, be cynical and even intimidate adults and having been predicted grade C in GCSE Maths – nobody thought that this "brute" was highly intelligent and could have been reasoned with.

The voices of those who were sympathetic and understanding of his struggles were muted by other pressures and concerns. The tipping point for the school was when Kushtrim threatened one of the senior staff members. Our storyteller now recounts what happened next and her own highly personalized response to events.

> Mr B. the Deputy Head, pulled me out of a Year 12 lesson to help him deal with . . . Kushtrim who was refusing to leave the school site. I knew it was serious. . . . There was urgency in Mr B's voice as he informed me that Kushtrim . . . had threatened Mr C., another Deputy Head, and then refused to be sent home. Mr B. assured me this was the best of all available options in following up Kushtrim's misbehaviour and paralysed my resistance by

describing the gravity of the situation, "If you don't make him leave now, I'll call the police."

. . . The day I was asked to send him off the school boundaries, the awareness that the school was exploiting his trust in me and was prepared to sacrifice it, weighed heavily on me. The task I was entrusted with went against everything I believed in and threatened to ruin my relationship with Kushtrim . . . I decided not to represent the institution, as it was failing both of us by denying us the right to be a student and an educator. He told me he wouldn't leave because he wanted to "go down, all the way". He said he was tired of fighting.

I asked him to leave because of me. I told him I wanted to represent his absent family in caring whether he got arrested or not. Then he said something that changed me forever, both as teacher and a person in the sense that it has fortified my altruistic beliefs and deepened my capacity to love and care for others, "When I got here they told me my tutor is a Serb. So I promised I will never talk to you because of what you did to my people. But you have been like a mother, the only friend I have here."

I didn't tell him I'm not a Serb because this misinterpretation showed the open-mindedness and magnanimity of this boy accused of being intolerant and vengeful. He knocked down his walls of prejudice, but we, the erudite and egalitarian educators, were left to deal with our school walls and the debate about who should come in and who should be denied access.

(Stabler 2011)

On one level, this story is an indictment of how a school, and the system of schooling, failed to understand a young person's needs. However, there is more to it than this. Schools find themselves at the epicentre of emotions, feelings and events from other worlds, other cultures. The challenges are complex and demanding. The Puerto Ricans of the Lower East Side proudly displayed their flag in the casita in their community garden. Kushtrim clung to his flag and a metal two-headed eagle which he wore around his neck. As his teacher said, 'It was all he had left from his country, the only familiar thing' for a boy in a strange and bewildering country.

Kushtrim's story is one of mutual misunderstanding and frustration. Kushtrim's teacher found herself at the centre of oppositional forces: having to make choices for herself about whose side she was on, and ultimately having to hold the ring. Once matters had escalated to the point where Kushtim was threatening, swearing and refusing to conform, there was only course of action left to the school – to exclude him. Caught between differing and opposing worlds and cultures, Kushtrim spiralled out of control and became another statistic: one of the excluded.

This leads us back to the heart of the challenge of leadership of place:

- What can school leaders do to respond to the needs of young people like Kushtrim?

- How can school leaders enable young people to feel that the school is a space which is enriching and empowering, and which helps them find their place in the world?

We bring to our experience of place our own history and culture. Our day-to-day encounters with others can make us feel that there is a place for us in a school or in the community, or they can make us feel alien to that place. Differences can be a source of interest and exploration, or a basis for misunderstanding. Where individuals and communities are separated and fearful of each other, confusion, and conflict become the order of the day. This was the case for the race riots in England in 2001, mentioned in the introduction.

Place on the agenda

The policy arena

The riots first took place in Oldham (which is part of Greater Manchester). At the time, Oldham had the highest number of race hate crimes in the Greater Manchester area, with some 1,133 racist crimes being reported in 2001–2002: a 75.4 per cent increase on the previous year. As an indicator of the degree of separation between the white and Asian communities, the rate of mixed-race marriage in the town was less than 1 per cent and both primary and secondary schools were predominantly single race (Guardian 2001).

The Cantle Commission of Inquiry, set up by Labour Home Secretary David Blunkett, examined the origins of the riots. It concluded that the towns were characterized by a high degree of polarization. Communities were segregated, typically living 'parallel' but separate lives. Trust had broken down and there were pressing issues about citizenship, diversity and opportunity which needed to be addressed to avoid further violence (Cantle 2001). While the physical segregation, in terms of housing, was not a surprise to the Inquiry team, the degree of polarization, and the ways in which it spread into people's daily lives, was. Educational arrangements, community and voluntary bodies, places of employment, places of worship, social and cultural networks were all separate and divided. In the view of the Inquiry team, this allowed opportunities for extremist groups on both sides of the divide to exert their influence.

The battle for space and place in these Northern towns entered the consciousness of politicians, and shaped the political debate and the policy agenda. Different worlds and different cultures collided, as they fought for resources, space and territory. Politicians were forced to recognize the impact of these collisions and to develop polices in response to them. The political concern was on the growing divisions in society and the rise of political extremism. The political imperative was to create greater *community cohesion* (Cantle 2001; Dyson and Gallannaugh 2008; Riley 2012).[4] Other high-profile events increased political concerns in the United Kingdom about community cohesion and place. Most notable among these were the London bombings in July 2005 (also known as 7/7): a series of suicide attacks carried out during London's rush hour by three Muslim Pakistani British men and a British citizen of Jamaican descent who had converted to Islam. Their declared motivation was opposition to Britain's involvement in the War in Iraq (HMSO 2006).

Community cohesion

The policy response to events by the then Labour Government included a re-appraisal of the role of the state, and the development of a strong community cohesion agenda which emphasized the centrality of public services. Launching the policy in 2007,

Alan Johnson described his understanding of community cohesion in the following terms:

> By community cohesion, we mean working towards a society in which there is a common vision and sense of belonging by all communities; a society in which the diversity of people's backgrounds and circumstances is appreciated and valued; a society in which similar life opportunities are available to all; and a society in which strong and positive relationships exist and continue to be developed in the workplace, in schools and in the wider community.[5]
>
> (DCSF 2007, p. 2)

Practical guidelines were introduced to support the development of community cohesion . Schools were assigned a distinctive role. A legal duty was placed on all maintained (publicly funded) schools in England to encourage community cohesion 'by promoting equality of opportunity and inclusion for different groups of pupils within a school and promoting shared values' (DCSF 2007, p.6).

Schools have long been expected to *build tolerance* between and within communities. However, with the emergence of the community cohesion agenda came the expectation that they should *challenge intolerance*. This has given school leaders community responsibilities that go far beyond educating students and has implications for how leadership is exercised, and policy is operated. Community engagement is hard (Berg et al. 2006). As was evident in Oldham, and elsewhere, communities do not necessarily bind together in a free and relaxed manner. Where communities are cohesive but diverse, they may merge or interconnect over time. Where there is intolerance or hostility, individual communities may tend to cling together.

Community cohesion is a relatively new policy direction in the United Kingdom, and its full implications are as yet unknown (Dyson and Gallannaugh 2008). However, the current policy debate fails to acknowledge the ways in which the values and beliefs of different groups and communities can be at variance with each other. There is lack of clarity about *whose* values should underpin cohesion and *what* communities should cohere around. The implicit assumption is that the task of the school is to harness networks and relationships in a locality for some common educational 'good'. Within this climate, the role of school leaders remains a critical but underexplored area.

The national focus on place and community cohesion led to a range of other policy initiatives, including the Preventing Violent Extremism Policy (also known as Prevent). Launched in 2007 to encourage local and national bodies to work together to prevent violent extremism, Prevent was a cross-department programme run by the Office for Security and Counter-Terrorism. Resources were targeted at local authorities with the largest Muslim populations and activities included how to teach school children how to spot a terrorist (Guardian 2008). The Prevent policy has been criticized by a leading Civil Liberties figure, Shami Chakrabarti, as being one of the biggest spying programmes in Britain in modern times (Guardian 2009).

A further policy development in 2008 was the introduction of an annual *Place Survey*. The Survey was designed to measure views about the extent to which people of different backgrounds get on well with one another in a locality. Resources were distributed on the basis of outcomes from the Survey. The more likely residents were to say that people did not get on well with one another, the higher the level of funding would be. Across London, the differences in response to this question have been significant, with less than 1 in 2 people in Barking and Dagenham believing that people get on well, compared with 3 out of 4 in Waltham Forest (Higham 2010).[6]

With the change in Government from a Labour to a Conservative-Liberal Coalition, community cohesion has remained an important political priority. In 2011, following a speech by Conservative Prime Minister David Cameron on multiculturalism, the Coalition Government announced a withdrawal in funding from some community groups deemed as being 'too soft on Islamic extremism' (Guardian 2011).

The policy environment

Within this emerging policy environment, place has emerged in many guises. For the urban planner, or architect, notions of *place and identity* have become central to discussions about the design of localities or the character of neighbourhoods (Hague and Jenkins

2005). The notion of leadership of place has also moved centre stage, becoming an important issue for policy makers, practitioners and researchers alike (Collinge et al. 2010).

In the public sector arena, *Leadership of place* signifies an expectation about the role of the formal leaders, such as councillors and local authority officials in shaping localities and generating social cohesion (Gibney, Yapp et al. 2009). At a policy level, the growing emphasis on place is connected to national policy aspirations to develop more integrated public services, by bringing economic development, planning, housing, regeneration, education, transport and health together on a locality basis (Benington and Hartly 2009).

In the next chapter, I go on to explore place and the city. The purpose of that exploration is to set the lives and experiences of individual young people such as Kustrim into a broader context. The chapter explores the patterns and factors that shape the lives of city dwellers today and highlights the impact of cities on their rural hinterlands. It examines the particular struggles that the poor and displaced face in making and maintaining a place for themselves in the city. To illustrate these issues, the chapter throws a spotlight on London, exploring what has changed over recent decades and examining the implications of these changes for young people, and for schools and their leaders.

Notes

1 Ireland was the first country to be mapped by ordinance survey maps.

2 Place and space are closely connected and are not only important but highly charged and contested issues. Space relates to 'history and identity' (Dillabough and Kennelly 2009, p. 6) and is associated with 'placelessness' that sense of loss of identify and cultural security that can exist in our cities (Eade 2000).

3 She was a Master's student at the Institute of Education, London, and wrote about '*Kushtrim*' as part of an assignment for a module I teach called *Leading in Diverse Cultures and Communities*.

4 Community cohesion has been defined as having five domains: common values; social order; social solidarity and reductions in wealth disparities; social networks and social capital; and attachment to place (Forrest and Kearns 2001, p. 8).

5 Alan Johnson, Secretary of State for Education and Skills, speaking in Parliament on 2 November 2006.

6 Negative perceptions appear to have been linked to factors such as, low levels of education, poverty and the numbers in the local population who had been born in Pakistan.

CHAPTER TWO

A place in the city?

At one time the nations of Europe confined the undesirable Jews in city ghettos. But to-day the dominant economic class, by less arbitrary but none the less rigorous methods, has confined the undesirable yet necessary workers into ghettos of remarkable meanness and vastness. East London is such a ghetto . . . where two million workers swarm, procreate, and die . . .

The People of the Abyss, JACK LONDON, 1903

Place and the city

Cities can be dangerous places for children and young people. But they can also be places of opportunity. Cities bear first witnesses to the social transformations of societies, acting as the interface between the poor, the aspirational, the established and the elite. Cities harbour great wealth and opportunities. However, they can also become battlegrounds for the distribution of power and resources. The urbanization of poverty is on the increase; about 1 in 3 of the world's urban population now lives on the edges of the cities of developing countries (UN-Habitat 2005). In the twenty-first century, the rural populations of sub-Saharan Africa, East and South-East Asia and South Africa congregate in the 'Dakars',

'Vientianes' or 'Cape Towns'. In South America, cities such as San Paulo and Rio di Janeiro have become melting pots which attract the creative as well as the displaced. In 1801, 75 per cent of Britain's 8 million population was rural. By 1901, 75 per cent of Britain's 40 million population was urban. Not only did city populations grow fast but also both rural migrants and immigrants flocked to industrial cities, such as Manchester, Leeds and London, seeking work, In 1903, Jack London wrote his vivid first-hand account of life in London's East End, *The People of the Abyss*. He stayed in workhouses and slept on the streets to experience London's 'underworld' and the conditions faced by the city's estimated half a million poor. The times of which he wrote, he reminded his readers, were considered 'good times' in England, and yet, 'the starvation and lack of shelter' which he encountered, in his view 'constituted a chronic condition of misery' which was never wiped out, even in the periods of greatest prosperity. While the conditions that Jack London wrote about no longer exist, as will be discussed in Chapter 5 the East End remains a place of extremes, with poverty and wealth juxtaposed against each other.

Our cities change fast. Impoverished downtown areas can become gentrified relatively quickly. New populations move in and established ones move out. In parts of our cities in South Africa, Britain and the United States, and across the globe, the struggle for a place – a home in the world – is powerful and intense. The societal shifts which emerge as a result of the social transformations of societies have a particular impact on our cities. As Mamphela Ramphele, the South African academic and anti-apartheid campaigner, argues, the dislocations brought about by social upheaval can be dysfunctional or productive. They can generate distrust and conflict, and a climate of violence and crime, or trigger the collapse of school systems. However, they also can lead to a culture of self-reliance and pride (Ramphele 2008).

In our globalizing world, social transformation has promoted a climate of mobility, change and, for some, insecurity. Indigenous communities across the globe have long fought to retain their ties to the land, or to the place of their forbears. For the city dweller, such links may be weak. City dwellers change location for a multiplicity of reasons. The upwardly mobile leave their place of birth to continue their education or seek advancement. With the fond hope of improving their lot, the poor, the displaced, the refugee and the economic migrant seek new prospects in our cities.

Cities represent opportunities and possibilities, not just problems. I think about the buzz in my own home city of Manchester, and the efforts of Manchester's Founding 'Fathers' to foster educational and social welfare opportunities for its citizens. I think too of the renaissance and resilience of other cities: Liverpool with its cheekiness and energy; London, my home for many years, with its vibrant, cosmopolitan communities and the highest rates of inter-ethnic marriages in the world; Chicago with its regeneration of new approaches to schooling; Sao Paulo with its flamboyance; New York reigniting its spark after the traumas of 9/11. Cities around the world attract large and diverse populations of incomers. They may be migrants from within their own countries seeking new economic opportunities, or immigrants from countries facing social, political or military upheaval. Many cities are maelstroms, whirlpools of excitement, energy and risk. They are places of fluidity, upheaval and change. They become focal points for societal struggles about the distribution of resources, epicentres for the overthrow of accepted social norms and seedbeds for the creation of new ideas. Conversely, they also serve as hubs for conservative forces seeking to maintain the influence of the elite, the wealthy and those seeking to preserve an old way of life.

Our cities are full of people seeking a place for themselves. However, contemporary global patterns of population movement add a new dimension to the meaning of place. The scale and speed of change are greater than ever before, bringing a growing diversity of groups into close proximity. *Communities may* coexist side by side but speak different languages, hold different beliefs, maintain different *values*. Thus, place assumes a particular intensity in our mobile and diverse communities where the values and beliefs of established and new communities can rub alongside or rub against one another, producing a kaleidoscope of social and political alliances or antagonisms.

The contradictions of our cities are endless: the cultural richness *versus* the day-to-day challenges of life in the inner city, or on social housing estates. For our schools there is the creativity and vibrancy of the children *versus* the unremitting pressures on our city teachers; the employment attractions of city life for business high flyers *versus* the difficulties faced by many city schools in attracting and retaining staff in the face of expensive housing and tough working conditions. These contrasts generate questions about how societies educate the children of the most deprived, in close proximity to those of the most advantaged. Nevertheless, many of the unique and positive attributes of city life have implications for the provision of education:

● Cities are key economic centres, with a diversity of economic and employment opportunities. Large cities have a rich and varied economic infrastructure which ensures a highly diversified workforce and significant opportunities for social and economic mobility.

● Cities – and primate cities, often capital cities – are centres of government, political and social activity which in its turn attracts a wide range of non-governmental organizations that require proximity to the centre of policy-making. Many primate cities have become a nexus of information, influence and lobbying.

● Major cities are almost invariably centres for education and the arts, with a disproportionate concentration of performing arts, galleries and museums and a self-reinforcing concentration of artistic and creative activity.

● Cities are centres of ethnic, linguistic and religious diversity, attracting a rich range of internal and external migrants who contribute to social, economic and cultural diversity (Riley and West-Burnham 2004, p. 5).

However, each context is different. Each city is unique – a mosaic of localities and neighbourhoods, each with its own distinctive characteristics. Many areas within our cities house diverse and complex communities which change in response to the movement of families, the shifting labour markets and global influences, such as the arrival of refugees and migrants.

Both geography and history help shape localities and how place is experienced in them. For example, Hounslow, in West London, is near Heathrow Airport which is a large international hub airport. This proximity has an impact on the flow of populations and on local communities. In one Hounslow secondary school that I visited, 1 in 8 pupils is a refugee or an asylum seeker. A hundred years ago the point of arrival to Britain would have been the Docklands of Estate London. Today it is the Airport. Many Hounslow families are closely tied to the Airport by employment. Children expect transience: parents returning to their country of origin or for a visit, relatives being granted, or denied, residence. Planes flying low overhead are a constant reminder of movement, travel, uncertainty and opportunity. Communities and families can become divided: those who are granted residency in their new country and those who are not.

Population movements reshape the city landscape. Within this fluid and dynamic framework, global events and developments have an increasingly significant impact on our cities and on our city schools. Children affected by political conflict in one country become refugees within other countries, arriving in their new and alien city often finding themselves in challenging schools which already serve disadvantaged, diverse and sometimes embattled communities. It becomes the role of these schools to serve as the interface between society and the emotional and economic pressures which characterize the lives of countless pupils and their families. Schools are often such families' only accessible link with the 'establishment'.

However, it is not only children who are refugees or migrants whose lives are shaped by mobility and transience. Kevin lives in Salford. His story was described to me in the following terms by John Evans, his headteacher, who had been involved in the project Leadership on the Front-line (see Chapter 3):

> Kevin is in year 6, first came to us in year 1, from a school over the road but we have now worked out that he has had thirteen moves. He left us and came back to us six times, and has been to seven other schools in between, usually because his mum is escaping the latest boyfriend who has turned violent. The only boyfriends I have known have all been drug users. We have done a lot of work with Kevin. I have done a lot of work with his mom. She herself has many many issues. She was brought up in Children's Home, but Kevin is an extremely sensitive boy and is quite embarrassed about the things that go on in his life. He takes his education seriously and has amazing general knowledge and I think his mum is actually a quite bright woman just fallen along the way.
>
> His mum is doing this TV programme. . . . I think the title was "My father won't give up drugs" and there is a DNA test

as to who is the father of the baby and he was proved to be the father. But when the programme came out Kevin had two days off school. Mum has not been near since the programme came on air. When Kevin came to school and he didn't know what to do and he knew that all the children had watched the programme and he didn't know what to say.

Thus, it is not only international flux, but also the dynamics of families struggling to function which can impinge on the lives of children and shape their sense of who they are. For schools, this adds yet another layer of complexity. Their understanding of how young people experience place not only has to take into account national and international issues, the broader context of the city and the distinctiveness of the locality, but also the encounters which touch children's lives every day.

Children also have to find their place in the school. Many of the young people involved in *Leadership on the Front-line* drew their school with love and relish, as is shown in Amber's depiction of the glorious rainbow gleaming above her London school (Illustration 2.1). Clearly, school is an important place for her.

But Amber also has to find her place in her locality. And her family has to find its place in the city.

ILLUSTRATION 2.1

The struggle to find a place in the city

Finding a place in the city is a particular challenge for the poor and the dispossessed. Socio-economic factors and political priorities have often been shown to have shaped housing and social policy decisions to the disadvantage of the poor and less powerful. In the 1950s, for example, many of the white indigenous communities in East London's Bethnal Green were often unwilling migrants to the suburbs and the new towns around London (Young and Wilmott 1957). In the 1960s, a similar story unfolded in Boston when members of the Italian-American community were forced to leave their tenements to make way for luxury housing (Gans 1962).

The political priorities of the established elites continue to limit the choices of the poor and less powerful, as was the case in the City of Westminster (a London borough). In the early 1980s, the council leader, Dame Shirley Porter, heiress to a supermarket chain fortune, spearheaded a scheme that was later shown in court to be a concerted effort to boost the election prospects of her Conservative Administration.

As part of the scheme, Westminster City Council sold off 500 council (publicly funded) homes each year to potential Conservative voters in marginal wards (localities for voting purposes). The council also removed homeless individuals and families with complex problems out of Westminster to the Home Counties outside London. When this route dried up homeless families were moved into wards that were already Labour voting. In 1989, more than 100 homeless families were removed from hostels in marginal wards and placed in high-rise buildings which were 'riddled' with asbestos (Blackhurst 1995).

The 'building stable communities' policy was ultimately declared illegal and Dame Porter was found guilty of 'wilful misconduct' and 'disgraceful and improper gerrymandering' (BBC 2004). She was accused by one of the Law Lords of deliberate, blatant and dishonest misuse of public power and a misuse of power 'not for the purpose of financial gain, but for that of electoral advantage. In that sense it was corrupt' (Magill 2001). In 2004, Dame Shirley was forced to pay £12m in settlement of a legal surcharge for her key role in, the policy, which, ironically, was called 'building stable communities'(BBC 2004).

The Westminster example demonstrates the extremes of policy and the limited options available to low income families to choose for themselves a *place called home*. More recent policy developments seem likely to continue this pattern of displacement of the poor and needy. Changes in housing policy are likely to have an impact on countless children and young people, particularly in London. They will be forced to leave their current homes and neighbouring schools. How many children and young people will be affected is as yet unknown. The only certainty is uncertainty. The scramble to find their place in the city will start afresh, in London and elsewhere.[1]

A place called London

Transience and transformation

London is dynamic. It has always been a city of transience and transformation. Nearly 1 in 3 of London's 7 million residents was born outside England. More than 300 languages are spoken by the people of London, and the city has at least 50 non-indigenous communities with populations of more than 10,000.[2] London's East End is now home to many second- and third-generation Bengali people, as well as immigrants from across the globe, and white working-class communities who have lived there for several generations (Riley and Stoll 2005).

Poverty and wealth, and stability and mobility have always been a part of London's story. For Jack London, the East End was *The City of Degradation*, a gigantic slum fostering a brutal way of life:

> The City of Dreadful Monotony the East End is often called, especially by well-fed, optimistic sightseers, who look over the surface of things and are merely shocked by the intolerable sameness and meanness of it all. If the East End is worthy of no worse title than The City of Dreadful Monotony, and if working people are unworthy of variety and beauty and surprise, it would not be such a bad place in which to live. But the East End does merit a worse title. It should be called The City of Degradation. . . . Sights and sounds abound which neither you

nor I would care to have our children see and hear is a place where no man's children should live, and see and hear. . . . For here, in the East End, the obscenities and brute vulgarities of life are rampant.

The East End of which he wrote was one of misery and degradation, of the poorest dying isolated and alone.

The mean streets merely look mean from the outside, but inside the walls are to be found squalor, misery, and tragedy. While the following tragedy may be revolting to read, it must not be forgotten that the existence of it is far more revolting. In Devonshire Place, Lisson Grove, a short while back died an old woman of seventy-five years of age. At the inquest the coroner's officer stated that "all he found in the room was a lot of old rags covered with vermin". He had got himself smothered with the vermin. The room was in a shocking condition, and he had never seen anything like it. Everything was absolutely covered with vermin . . .

Nevertheless, despite these observations of the East End as 'a ghetto, where the rich and the powerful do not dwell, and the traveller cometh not', the East End had one jewel: its children.

I have talked with these children, here, there, and everywhere, and they struck me as being as bright as other children, and in many ways even brighter. They have the most active little imaginations. Their capacity for projecting themselves into the realm of romance and fantasy is remarkable. A joyous life is romping in their blood. They delight in music, and motion, and colour . . . The children of the Ghetto possess all the qualities which make for noble manhood and womanhood; but the Ghetto itself, like an infuriated tigress turn[s) on its young . . .

Much has changed since Jack London's day. He would certainly be surprised by London's diversity. However, his description of London's children resonates. Despite the socio-economic challenges, London's schools are vibrant places, marked by the energy and creativity of the children.

London today

As a city of culture, London embraces the lifestyles and beliefs of citizens from across the globe (Block 2006; Cohen 1997; Hannerz 1996; Kearney 2008; Sassen 2001). Yet in some ways, the notion of 'London' is a mythical one. London is a city of villages and disparate communities, with some very desirable countrified hamlets and scattered areas of urbanicity. The London experienced by the urban elite is rarely the one familiar to young people in London's state school system. It is a city in which the most affluent conduct their lives in close proximity to some of the most needy (Grace 1978, 2006). Many young people do not perceive themselves as living in London but as in a locality – Greenwich, Hackney, Brent. For them London is Oxford Circus – a place you go to shop.

London is ethnically, linguistically, racially and religiously diverse. Based on children aged 0–15, greater London is the most ethnically diverse region in the United Kingdom (see Figure 2.1) and one of the most diverse cities in the world. Given the constant ebb and flow of communities and the constancy of change, the notion of what it means to be a Londoner is being redefined every day.

The majority (62%) of England's young black and black British population (aged 0–15) and almost a third (31%) of the Asian and Asian British population live in London see Figure 2.2 (ONS 2007).

However, there are significant differences across London's 32 boroughs. For example, the 0–15 population in Havering is around 86 per cent white, while more than 60 per cent of those in Tower

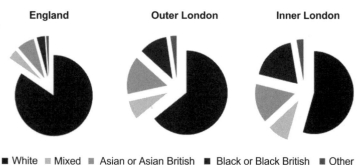

FIGURE 2.1 *London's Diversity.*

Asian or Asian British   Black or Black British

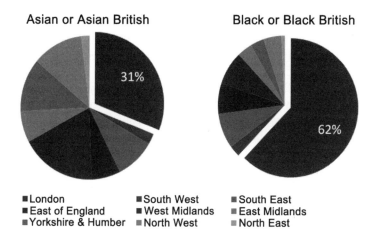

■London   ■South West   ■South East
■East of England   ■West Midlands   ■East Midlands
■Yorkshire & Humber ■North West   ■North East

FIGURE 2.2 *Black & Black British and Asian or Asian British.*

Hamlets, Newham and Brent are from other ethnic groups (ibid; Riley 2010). Historically, London has been very different from most other European cities, in that its poor and minority groups tend to live in the inner city, while the white and the wealthy live in the periphery. In Europe it is usually the opposite. However, the racial population balance between inner and outer London is now shifting, with a growing white population in the centre, and more minority ethnic groups moving to outer boroughs. As a consequence of these population shifts, as well as the changes in housing benefit, discussed earlier, for the first time, an increasing proportion of the capital's poor live in outer-London rather than inner-London.

Almost half of the children in inner-London are living in poverty, making inner-London the UK region with the highest rates of child poverty (Poverty Profile 2009). Taking into account housing costs, London's child poverty rates are the highest in the United Kingdom. The three-year period, 2004–07 saw 41 per cent of London's children living below the poverty line, compared with 30 per cent nationally. The ongoing squeeze on part-time work in London raises issues for lone parents searching for such jobs as well as for students from low-income families seeking to support their studies. Children of lone parent families are particularly vulnerable to poverty and there are large numbers of them in Barking and Dagenham, Hackney, Haringey, Newham and Islington. Although inner-London is worse than any English region on many indicators, it has seen improvements in recent years. Outer-London, however in contrast, has experienced a significant deterioration across a number of indicators, including child and working-age poverty.

Young Londoners today

Jack London's account of London's East End a century ago showed the stark impact of poverty on a community. Poverty remains an issue in London, today, although a very localized one. The ways in which young people experience London is also very localized. The communities they live in, go to school in, pass through on their way to important events and activities all influence how they experience life on the streets, on the tubes, on the buses. Their ethnicity, class, gender all shape daily interactions.

Schools need to know who the young people are, what they experience and what they think, if they are to meet the needs of today's children and young people (Riley 2010). As part of some work aimed at trying to understand the lives of young Londoners, I worked with colleagues at the Institute of Education to explore what young Londoners thought about the city's diversity. We took findings from an indicative survey of around 1,000 young Londoners carried out in 2004 and again in 2009 by the Greater London Authority and analysed it in greater depth. We found that when young Londoners were asked the question, 'What, if anything, would you say are the two or three best things about living in London?' The proportion selecting 'The mixture of people who live here' had increased significantly between 2004 and 2009 (see Figure 2.3).

Our first reflection was that this seemed like a success story for community cohesion. The London-wide findings also backed up other more localized studies[3] and tallied with my own research on the lives and experiences of young Londoners which indicated how much they enjoyed the diversity in their own schools. This was particularly so in areas where ethnic groups were relatively segregated along housing lines. Illustration 2.2 depicts one girl's positive views about the diversity in her school. 'All different, all equal', she says.

Across the two years of the Survey, we found that the young people most likely to be positive about London's diversity were from Indian and black groups. White and mixed ethnic groups were

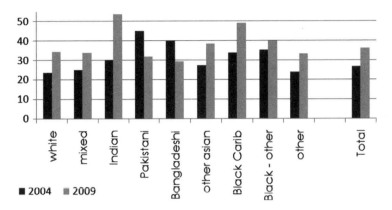

FIGURE 2.3 *'The mixture of people is one of the best things about London' (by ethnicity).*

ILLUSTRATION 2.2

the least likely to choose the mixture of people as being one of the best things about London, followed by young people from the Caribbean. Young women were more positive than men and while the young white British people surveyed were less positive than other groups, this situation had improved significantly between 2004 and

2009. We also found that where young white Londoners lived in social housing in London's ethnically diverse Council Estates, they were as likely to select 'the mixture of people who live here' as being important to them as non-whites (Riley 2010).

However, not all groups felt more positive about diversity in 2009 than they had five years earlier. The Pakistani and Bangladeshi young people surveyed in 2009 felt less positive about London's diversity a finding which raises important questions about place and identity, and divided communities.

- *Do London's Pakistani and Bangladeshi young people feel more vulnerable, more exposed to the scrutiny of others and the hostility of some?*

The answer to that question is – maybe. However, we simply don't have enough information to answer the question. What we do know is that young Asians are more likely than their white or black peers to say that they are aware of local tensions (Waltham Forest 2007) and to state that they feel they have been discriminated against because of their ethnicity, or religion (Ipsos Mori 2008).

Knowing young people's views about diversity is critical for schools. Equally important is to understand their views about the extent to which they feel they can influence decisions that affect their live. A 2007 survey in Waltham Forest found, for example, that only 1 out of 2 young white people thought they could influence the way things were run at school, compared with 3 out of 5 young Black people and 4 out of 5 young Asians. These differences between the groups were mirrored in their perceptions about the extent to which they could influence decision-making in their local area, with only 1 out of 5 white young people believing they could influence decisions, compared to 2 out of 5 young Black people and 1 out of 2 of young Asians (Waltham Forest 2007).

This chapter has thrown up a number of examples of the ways in which children and young people can experience a city divided. This matters to young people in a number of ways. Perceived and actual differences created by power, money, gender, ethnic origin not only shape daily encounters but also future beliefs and possibilities. If young people are to gain from living in the city, and contribute to what that city can become, they need to feel that they can shape it.

In London, some young white people feel that they cannot influence decisions about their lives, whether at school or in their locality. Some young Asians feel they have been discriminated against because of their ethnicity, or religion. Thus, creating bridges across communities and localities is not an optional extra for school leaders, but an essential activity. However, finding out what young people think and experience is more than bridging the gap between schools and communities. It is also a recognition of what they have to teach us. As Shukra et al. (2004, p. 192) argue, young people are:

. . . living and to some degree fashioning what it means to live in a multi-ethnic society at the level of their everyday experience be it in the playground, neighbourhood or youth club. It may just be that they have a more informed sense of how to live in a multicultural world than is often appreciated.

Chapter 3 shows some of the ways that we can learn from young people. It draws on information from some 70 schools involved in the *project Leadership on the Front-line* which examined some of the complexities of context and place. This exploration is made through the eyes of young people as well as through those of school leaders.

Notes

1 In 2010, the new Conservative-Liberal Coalition Government directed the policy headlight towards people living in privately rented property who were in receipt of government housing benefit. This is paid to defray the high rental costs of accommodation, particularly in central London. The policy intent was to reduce the government spending in a time of recession. The anticipated impact of the policy is that 17,000 people from low income families in central London will be forced to leave their subsided housing for cheaper accommodation in the outer areas of the city making London a more socially, ethnically and economically divided city. The policy has sparked a number of reactions, including Conservative Mayor of London, Boris Johnson, who has raised his spoken out against the possibility of a 'Kosovo-style cleansing' of the poor (BBC, 2010).

2 This is based on Census data for 2001 (Guardian 2008).

3 Such as one in Camden, which found that seven out of ten young people socialized with people of a different ethnic background on a regular basis, which was almost twice the proportion among adults aged 18 or over (37%) (Ipsos Mori 2008, p. 110).

CHAPTER THREE

Is this place always changing?

London, Liverpool, Birmingham, Cardiff, Manchester and Belfast

What's happening here (in Birmingham) is pretty interesting in terms of social engineering. It's ethnic cleansing in a way . . . What they're doing is destroying the community. There are generations of families being separated. The daughter's got a house down there . . . and now the daughter's being moved away. And what they've done is they've separated that link. And sometimes, those communities need those links. The structure of the family unit – they've destroyed that. And that's going to create social problems.

Headteacher, *Leadership on the Front-line*, SUNEIL, 2008

In this chapter, I want to explore the complexities of context and place. My aim is to demonstrate to school leaders the importance of scanning the local environment and keeping abreast of any changes. The two questions to keep in the forefront are: How do any changes in the locality, housing, new residents affect the communities? How do they affect the life of the school?

In the quotation which starts this chapter, Suneil, a London headteacher visiting Birmingham, reflects on the city's changing landscape. While inner-city regeneration creates all sorts of opportunities, it still tends to leave the most vulnerable in society behind, or dilutes their sense of place. Place is critical for those who have been forced to move away from their homes, or for those who have been left behind when their families or neighbours have gone. The place that individuals inhabit profoundly affects their sense of self. Brian Friel's work, Mamphela Ramphele's powerful book *A Bed called Home*, John Ogbu's focus on involuntary minorities, and Kushtrim's painful story all serve to demonstrate this point.

Place is something that touches our psyche, connecting with our sense of history and identity. Just think about gang battles over street corners, or Nationalists who burn the homes of incomers. Our ability to find a place to live, a place to work and a place to go to school is shaped by political and economic decisions, or historical circumstances, most of which are beyond the control of the poor or dispossessed. This lack of control creates a sense of powerlessness and alienation among the marginalized and disadvantaged groups, and this feeling is exacerbated when they see themselves as groups vying for resources, space or territory.

The magnitude of these issues was brought home to me when I carried out a review of education in London which involved interviewing some 30 headteachers across 6 London boroughs, as part of a wider study on the challenges for London leadership (Riley and West-Burnham 2003). The interviewees' concerns about the ever-pervading social and economic hardships that shape young people's lives dominated their stories:

> Children face great difficulties themselves and when they are in a housing crisis, or a family breakdown, then those problems pour into the school. . . . We have a high proportion of one parent families, often mothers who are low paid, and work long hours.

{Pupils} come to school in the morning with tales of such appalling experience at home, that they are simply not able to learn. . . . There are often massive disputes among some of the multi-relationship families, and the children bring these disputes into school with them.

They strove to understand the feelings and reactions of young people who had fled from violent conflict in their own countries:

Dealing with children from a war-torn country demands specific skills and knowledge . . . I try to keep abreast with events in Somalia and Bosnia. Sheer ignorance is one of my major problems. Children who come from war-torn countries often bring their anger and violence with them. A boy will suddenly pull out a knife to settle a minor dispute.

And they gave examples of the ways in which some young people 'inherited' disputes from their families:

In the streets around the school there are territorial gang wars between groups of Bangladeshi youths, and every trivial incident or insult leads to payback threats.

My later work with school leaders in the research and development project *Leadership on the Front-line* enabled me to see that attempting to define the common features of schools in challenging urban contexts could lead to unhelpful oversimplifications. It was important to try and understand the unique features of each school as well as the commonalities across schools.

Leadership on the Front-line focused on school leadership in challenging urban contexts. It ran from 2003 to 2009 and provided insights into the important contextual features which shape the lives of many disadvantaged communities (Riley et al. 2005; Riley 2008a, 2008b). More than 70 headteachers and principals took part, and came from a range of schools in challenging city contexts across the United Kingdom and Eire – Belfast, Birmingham, Cardiff, Dublin, London, Liverpool, Londonderry, Manchester and Salford, as well as schools in the Paris *banlieues*. The project included nursery, primary, secondary and special schools and reflected the different types of schools in UK and Eire city contexts including: denominational, integrated (Irish schools for both Catholic and Protestant children), single sex and co-educational.

The development of the project was stimulated not only by concerns about gaps in understanding about the contextual challenges of city schools, but also by a recognition of the importance of developing a more focused community-based approach to leadership. Discussions of context typically focus on measurable demographic or socio-economic features, such as population density, poverty and unemployment, identifying the conditions and locations of the poorest in our societies. In England, for example, the poorest communities are found in inner areas of our cities, industrial areas, in seaside towns and in isolated industrial towns which have lost their industrial base, such as mining areas. Housing is predominantly social housing or rented property, rather than privately owned, and is located in areas which are substantially disadvantaged, not only in terms of family circumstances but also neighbourhood deprivation which could include run-down facilities, as well as vandalism, high crimes rates and racist attacks (Turnstall et al. 2011).

Leadership on the Front-line offered a novel perspective on what it meant to be a headteacher in a city school: the day-to-day challenges, the pace and the complexity, all intensified by community contexts which were demanding and volatile, where, for example, young people might be subject to a dispersal order, a court order requires them to be under curfew after a certain hour of the day. By looking at these contextual challenges, I began to recognize the importance of adopting a more discriminating understanding of context and situation: the flow of populations of immigrants and refugee groups set against the background of the local history, economy and geography. But I began to think more about *place* than *context*. For me, the notion of *place* captured not only the physical and socio-economic conditions but also how individuals and communities identified themselves and responded to these circumstances and how they felt they could shape them.

In the next section, I draw on interviews and illustrative materials from nine headteachers and school principals involved in Leadership *on the Front-line*. They are from London, Liverpool, Birmingham, Cardiff, Manchester and Belfast. My purpose is to demonstrate the complexity of these contextual explorations and to discuss the difference between leading in context and leadership of place.

Seeing it and living it: Headteachers and school principals

London

What is particularly striking about the contexts of most of the *Leadership on the Front-line* schools is the speed of change, for example, in the composition of a school, as the following comments from Rachel a secondary headteacher in Greenwich in London demonstrate:

> Until about three years ago, we had 32 per cent bilingual pupils and about 46 per cent children from minority ethnic groups. . . . We've gone up to nearly 47 per cent bilingual pupils and 60 per cent-plus minority ethnic groups.

And the intensity of the social challenges, as described by a neighbouring primary headteacher in Woolwich, South London, Bob:

> (The school) is in one of the poorest wards in England. We have a very diverse community and have something like 39 different languages in the school and significant numbers of Black African children, particularly Somali children, a number of Vietnamese children, a range of Spanish speaking children and increasing children from Eastern Europe (we have Kosovan children in the school).
> Unemployment is a significant factor, mental health and housing issues have become significant as well. . . . Last year . . . we had a lot of difficulty amongst children and parents, bringing community issues and troubles from the estates into the school and carrying on the quarrels here.
> Other things are racism – where families have felt threatened through racism. Quite a lot of single parent families or families whose accommodation is inadequate a number of children and issues about having to sleep in the same room as parents and children having to share beds . . . that's not uncommon, its part and parcel of the poverty in the area.

The complexity and intensity of these issues raise major and long-term challenges for schools, as Bob commented:

It takes years of work to overcome the fears and resistance from parents who probably haven't been welcomed by a whole range of authority figures.

In order to make sense of this complexity, I drew on interview data from the project to develop a mapping tool which would capture the dimensions of local communities. The tool has four axes: *population* (stable or mobile e.g. with refugees and immigrants), *community profile* (single or multiple communities), *levels of engagement* (engaged with education or disengaged) and *community identity* (integrated with a strong community identity, or fragmented with disparate communities).

Liverpool

As part of the project, heads and principals mapped the community contexts of their schools, for example, Figure 3.1, mapped by Joan a headteacher from Liverpool. This infant school (for children aged 3–7), stands in an economically deprived area with high levels of unemployment. It is a transient community, with growing numbers of migrants and asylum seekers, characterized by high levels of pupil mobility.

Joan went on to describe the community in the following terms:

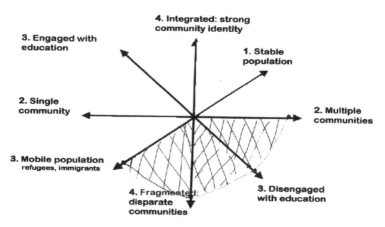

FIGURE 3.1 Liverpool School *(serving multiple disadvantaged communities).*

It's a very dysfunctional community, really I think. It's coming to the bottom of a very deep hole of deprivation, problems with drugs, arms, related crime. A lot of disaffected youth in gangs, children between 10 and 16 or 17 maybe. Causing a lot of problems for the people living here. . . . I've been a head here for 9 years, but I worked here some years before – a very stable area and in the time that I've been here, I've seen it go down and down, possibly due to the housing policy here where housing is being used to decant people who are having difficulties but the effect has been to move people out of this area who were very stable. Into that mix, I think, comes a lot of people just recently, asylum seeking families, who are having quite a lot of difficulty here.

It's quite a racist area, but there is a lot of short-term housing here. So currently in the school, I think, it's 19 per cent of the children are from asylum seeking families. The mobility rate here is 41 per cent – it's very high . . . There are 17 different languages amongst that group, but what we're finding is that people are coming in and going out, some of them because economically, they are moving around the area. That tends to be Czech Roma families, but there are other families who really are finding it very difficult to come to terms with the aggression.

Birmingham

Both the mapping exercise and school leaders' descriptions of context drew attention to the diversity and distinctiveness of school communities and served as a reminder of the importance of avoiding generic oversimplifications. Some schools served relatively homogenous communities, others much more diverse ones. The communities represented in a school could live close by, or some distance away. The school might be located in an area which does not reflect the socio-economic circumstances of its students, as seen in the following example from a Birmingham: secondary school, as described by headteacher David:

We are the first step out as receivers of the urban doughnut so we're in lovely grounds and Mosley which is nearby is one of the more affluent pleasant bits of central Birmingham. However, 70 per cent of our pupils come from the top 2 per cent areas of deprivation across the European community . . . 76 per cent are in the poorest quintile of society by multiple deprivation figures. . . .

We have an incredible diversity in terms of economic background, class. I have the son of a member of the House of Lords, and a government minister and I have 35 per cent Muslim community predominantly Pakistanis but some Bengali . . . Generally, Muslim families come from backgrounds of very low literacy levels and with a deficit starting point. We also have some very needy white working -class families . . . Significantly, the families come from very different areas so we have an official catchment area of 3.2 km which for a dense urban area is quite big but actually we have quite a lot of youngsters who come from outside that circle . . . And so there is a lack of identity on our campus.

The project helped me understand that communities could be socially and economically deprived but still rich in opportunities. It gave me a greater appreciation of the ways in which the mix and complexity of the socio-economic and ethnic create distinctive sets of challenges for school leaders. For example, schools on public housing estates on the outer rim of cities such as Cardiff, London, Manchester or Dublin serve white working-class communities that have moved from traditional inner-city areas. Employment opportunities for many of the residents are typically limited, local services sparse and buses into the centre of the city, irregular. Parental disenchantment with schools can be an issue, largely stemming from their own poor educational experience.

Cardiff

Claire, a headteacher of a Cardiff secondary school, drew Figure 3.2 to depict the context of the school she led which is located in Cardiff's Ely Estate.

She went on to describe the school in the following terms:

It takes its catchment from one indigenous location. It's predominantly an estate, so you've got a very similar homogenous catchment area . . . There's a strong identity of all the pupils with this area geographically . . . There are sections of the community

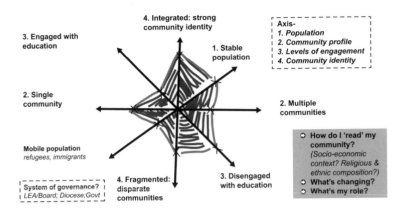

FIGURE 3.2 *Estate School, Cardiff.*

who create difficulties . . . When I arrived, the school's playing fields were littered with burnt out cars and there was damage done to the building . . . It's predominantly white working-class, although I don't like the term.

The challenges she identified, in terms of the lack of aspiration of white working-class communities are far from new in the education literature. They resonate with long-standing observations about class and schooling. For example, Willis' commentary on the oppositional cultures of some white working-class boys to the middle-class culture and the aspirations of school (Willis 1977), Bernstein's observations about fundamental differences in values (Bernstein 1977), and Angela McRobbie's analysis of the alternative cultures and expectations of white working-class girls (McRobbie 1991). Claire went on to add:

There's an element of aggression and quite a volatile element, and also (a) diffidence which is sometimes masked . . . Sometimes there is a naivety that goes alongside a streetwise approach. It seems a contraction, a paradox . . . A very small percentage go on to Higher Education . . . There's a lot of dysfunctional families, but I've noticed over the past few years that the affluence has increased slightly and there is a little more employment. . . . You've got older pockets, so you do get lots of grandparents taking on the role of the sensible parent . . . A feature of these types of parents is the total irrationality . . . in terms of responding (to issues). Pupils go home with stories and there is quite a significant number who will question you on very spurious evidence . . . Litigation is never far from some of them.

Manchester

This description strongly resonates with the comments of a South Manchester headteacher, Richard, whose secondary school is in an area with poor transport links and, until recently, a shaky social infrastructure:

> It's 52 per cent free school meals. We serve the poorest, officially the most socially deprived ward in England . . . So we've got severe urban poverty . . . but in terms of cleverness, we actually do get some of our brightest children from x (the most deprived ward). They really, really are bright kids . . . In terms of the estate, its 70,000 housing units . . .
>
> If you want to talk about an inverted snobbery form of evaluating how tough the context is here . . . one of our ex-students was murdered. He left school two years ago last summer and we had his friend who was shot dead just before Christmas . . . One of our parents was killed in a motorcycle accident. So there seems to be lots of deaths in the area. For the last 4 years, every summer I've gone to a funeral, to do with our children.
>
> The crime rate is high, there is a drugs problem, but we do have squirrels on the ground, we do have our own pond. But it is a tough community. It is white working-class, we have about 1 per cent from different ethnic groups, very few, less than 10 per cent but it is on the increase, because they're pulling down flats and building these start-up homes . . . Some families are moving in. There are fewer problems with money, but there is considerable disaffection and underachievement.

Colin, the headteacher of a boys' school in North Manchester had a very different set of challenges: a very needy but far-flung community. The distance of families from the school made it hard to understand the complex needs of the students, or to reach out to their families:

We serve a big catchment area in the north of the city and I think we have about 41 feeder schools . . . We've got some of the most deprived areas in the country in our catchment area . . . It's challenging. . . and on top of that you've got boys' school . . . we've got 55 statemented students [those with a 'statement' of special educational needs] which is big. The biggest problem in addressing the deprivation is undoubtedly the distance pupils are from the school. Many of our neediest kids come from furthest away . . . and they've got a 4 mile trip to school. So that's a big issue.

The other thing is that in geographical terms we're quite remote even from the community. . . . It's not like my previous schools where there was this great comprehensive stuck in the middle of a big estate on the top of the hill and visually, and geographically, it was a focus. It's not like that. So we've got to try to engage our community by remote control. We do it through home–school liaison and through working with primary schools. But it is extremely difficult to do it in a meaningful way. Even working with primary schools and that many primary schools, it's difficult because the kids are dispersed so far and wide.

Belfast

The final two extracts included in this chapter to illustrate the complexities of context are from Northern Ireland. Both schools are located in areas with relatively stable populations. The first extract describes the context of a nursery school in West Belfast serving a Catholic community. The school is located on a public housing estate which has high male unemployment and has been adversely affected by civil unrest. Parent literacy is low but, in the view of Marianne the principal, the community is starting to resurrect itself and the school feels part of this regeneration:

The Parish is on an estate which, in the last 30 years, has seen a lot of civil unrest. People feel they have been dumped on, first by society, in terms of lack of services in the community, then by the 'Brits' as they would call them, and then the police, and also by the paramilitaries because this area saw a lot of tension and rows and stuff . . . But in the last 5 or 6 years, I have witnessed a change in the sense that instead of looking inwardly, the community has started to look outwardly a bit.

You find in this area that a lot of them would be born here, marry here and die here. They do their shopping here even though things are much more expensive because John M. up there would do 'tick' in terms of benefits. It's not any money lending or anything but I mean they drink in there, [local pub] is about a 10 min walk. It's a very inward looking community, but since Father x came here he's sort of got them geed up . . . And in partnership with all of us, the schools and the community organizations and the church, there has been a drive to say 'hold on a minute we matter here' and 'look we are all not dossers and a lot of us want to work and a lot of us want peace so what can we do?'

Marianne believed that as a leader, she needed to challenge the gender stereotypes prevalent in the community:

Male unemployment is still very high and the women work part-time jobs. Women would be the main bread earners, greater earners, but for some reason it seems to be a very male dominated environment in terms of attitudes. We have women coming in here who would like to do courses but saying 'he wouldn't let me'. We would say 'why do you have to ask him?' and she would reply 'because I would have to ask him'. Some of the men in this area would see women being educated as a bit of a threat to themselves.

This final extract, from Anna, a Belfast secondary headteacher, captures the social consequences for a community when civil unrest is combined with ongoing deprivation:

The school originally would have served the area of T. which was a new housing estate developed in the 1960s. At that time, it was an area basically that was to house people who had been burnt out, frightened out of their original area. Certainly during the 1970s, it was a very fragmented community because there was no ownership, no community feel, as well as that there was no infrastructure . . . shopping centre. So people at that time . . . were very poorly served and it was also on the outskirts of West Belfast. . . .

It's now a more settled environment. . . . The area would be in the top 10 per cent of wards with multi-deprivation . . . and the social/economic deprivation is severe. Within the school itself, which is the only secondary school in this particular area. . . . We have over 70 per cent free school meals.

The extracts that have been included so far highlight issues about class, race, ethnicity and gender:

- *Class*: white working-class families, some of whom hold negative views of education, others who are beginning to say, 'hold on a minute we matter here'

- *Race and Ethnicity*: refugees who experience racism or hostility, immigrant families who value education and have high aspirations for their children

- *Gender*: women who are the breadwinners and who still feel they have to defer to the men in their households

The extracts raise issues about identity and belonging. How do young people see themselves? How do they feel about their lives? The next section goes on to answer those questions from the perspective of the young people themselves.

Seeing it and living it: Students

One of *Leadership on the Front-line's aims* was to examine the extent to which widening school leaders' knowledge and understanding about children's lives might enable them to develop fresh perspectives on what schools could offer. Groups of pupils from all of the schools in the second and third phases of the project were interviewed: nearly 500 children aged 3–17 in 49 schools. We asked two broad questions:

- *What is it like living round here?*
- *What is it like being in this school?*

Pupils were encouraged to draw pictures which illustrated their experience of life within the wider community and within the school community. These images provided powerful insights into the complexities of their lives, as the following section illustrates.

What's it like living round here?

In their day-to-day lives outside school, young people had to contend with difficulties ranging from rubbish and poor street lighting to threats of violence and unstable families. Their lives could be constrained by lack of play space, fears for safety and worries about gangs. Sometimes they were confronted with prejudice or low expectations of their abilities and possibilities. But for many, life was enhanced by different languages, cultures, foods, beliefs and expectations. They had the support of friends and families and opportunities for sports, cultural events and social activities: see Illustration 3.1 drawn by a young woman from South London. The drawing exemplifies the contrast between the world of the school and the world of the street. The locality is unsafe, and children are afraid of gangs and crime. And yet there is the richness of family life, large family weddings to attend with vibrant music and laughter. The school provides a place for different voices to be heard and for friendship 'a chance to be yourself' and to learn about new worlds 'in the film club'.

The young people we interviewed experienced their area of the city in all its complexities. They were likely to know about drugs and violence but equally, they knew about the opportunities. Children from Newham in East London knew the Olympics would bring a buzz to their home territory along with new facilities; Manchester children knew about the Library Theatre, Old Trafford (the home

ILLUSTRATION 3.1

of the Reds), Birmingham children, Symphony Hall and Edgbaston, the home of cricket in the Midlands, a draw for Birmingham's white, Asian and Afro-Caribbean communities.

Images of guns and drugs were replicated in a number of drawings such as Illustration 3.2 drawn by Ameini, a girl a school in East London. The contrast between street life and school life is stark.

Children and young people have a clear and sophisticated understanding of territory – their territory and that of others – and how to manage and survive in it. We found that their lives were constrained by their views of what was familiar and safe and what wasn't. They understood boundaries: this is my estate where people know me and I feel safe. Here are the areas whether others have left their mark. This awareness of boundaries restricted their views about where they felt free to walk, cycle and take public transport.

Public transport could be dangerous: a bus going into a hostile neighbourhood, local tube stations used by drug dealers, areas which gangs had tagged (drawn their gang-related graffiti to establish their territory). Many of our city children do not travel any significant distance from their homes, often feeling unsafe and vulnerable outside the known and familiar area – and they appeared to have grown more worried about travelling after the July 2005 bombings.

However, living close to a tube line could also create a sense of possibilities and opportunities. The same was true for young people

ILLUSTRATION 3.2

who lived near the city centre in Manchester and Birmingham. Yet, proximity and access are different. Young people living in Dublin's social housing estates travelled to the city centre, but to shop, rather than to take advantage of any other cultural or social resources. The Celtic tiger appeared to have left some families behind.

What's it like being in this school?

When we asked young people what it was like for them in their school, it became clear that space and territory loomed as large in school as out of it. What mattered for them was that the school provided the opportunity to be themselves: to run around, to play with friends, to explore, to develop – their thinking and their skills. When schools offered a range of clubs and activities, pupils valued it. They also appreciated a well thought-out learning environment. These issues emerge strongly in the locality studies which follow this chapter.

The playground is one of the most important aspects of school life for many children, particularly the youngest. It is one of the few places where they can run around and play with their friends and be safe. Schools which have created exciting play areas which are rich with opportunities for exploration have massively enriched children's lives. In Illustration 3.3, a young pupil from a

ILLUSTRATION 3.3

North Manchester school drew with evident delight the school's three playgrounds: the quiet playground, the ball playground and the games playground.

Friendships were an important aspect of school for children of all ages. For older children in co-educational schools, it was important and enjoyable to be able to be friends with someone of the opposite sex – an issue raised by a number of Asian children. Children in schools which are very mixed racially, ethnically and socially value diversity and school-based friendships across cultures and communities (see Illustration 3.4).

Seeing school and community through the eyes of young people enabled school leaders involved in the project to understand children's lives in the round and the complexities of community. The interviews with students enriched the leaders' understanding

ILLUSTRATION 3.4

about the intricacies of their lives – disjunctures between school and community; anxieties about safety and space; links between place and identity. The ways in which communities are perceived by outsiders may be very different from the perceptions of insiders (in this case, the young people themselves). An understanding of these issues helps for school leaders to manage and negotiate the interface between schools and communities.

From leading in context to leadership of place

Leadership on the Front-line illustrated the tensions and dilemmas experienced by school leaders in responding to different beliefs, cultures and value systems. It revealed much about the leaders themselves: what motivated them; what helped them learn; what unleashed their creativity. School leaders involved in the project concluded that:

- Being a leader in a challenging context was about passion, beliefs and possibilities.

- It required new ways of working that cut across conventional boundaries; it was about making connections rather than directing events.

- School leaders often lacked the tools to do this systematically in ways that could unleash their creativity and potential and that of their students.

The challenges presented by their communities could be daunting for these urban leaders. They often felt overwhelmed by the relentless pressures and saw themselves as standing in the front line in defence of social justice:

- fighting for what is right for children and families
- protecting the community
- promoting children's physical and mental well-being
- serving the community of which they are a part
- recognizing the potential of children

- showing 'it can be different here'
- being committed to inner-city children
- encouraging the school to be a moral community

We realized that what school leaders in challenging contexts have to know and be able to do, may well be what their counterparts in less pressing contexts will have to know and be able to do in future years. The ethnic, cultural and socio-economic changes that are first felt in our cities and socially disadvantaged areas are likely to affect societies as a whole at some point down the line.

School leaders' most powerful learning from *Leadership on the Front-line* was recognizing the need to take a broader perspective on leadership and to reach *beneath*, *beyond* and *within* the micro-politics of the school:

- *Reaching beneath* was about understanding the forces, experiences and relationships which influence children or staff to act in particular ways. The focus on children's lives and experiences, and on the complexities of the communities in which they live, spurred many project participants to find out more about what 'community' means in general and in their own particular circumstances, and to bring their knowledge back into the life of the school.

- *Reaching beyond* was a striving to see the wider picture: what young people experience and what they can achieve and be in their lives – and who can help them get there. For many participants, this reaching beyond was a reaffirmation of the importance of working with parents and communities, and a determination to find new ways to do this.

- *Reaching within* was about reconnecting to the inner drivers: the values which shaped their core attitudes and beliefs. Participants shared a common view that they needed to return to these core purposes and make them more explicit in their day to day encounters and actions. They also acknowledged the need to take the time to reaffirm the personal values which underpin their leadership.

The project confirmed my views about the ways in which context and community shape leadership. The contextual challenges for school leaders included understanding the ways in which urban communities can and do change; developing strategies for creating a closer alignment between schools and communities; and managing conflict and complexity.

However, engaging in a very different dialogue and debate with communities is a difficult enterprise. It goes beyond reaching out to help the community. It is about learning from – and making better use of – existing local resources. This is an issue Karen Seashore Louis and I explored in a review of schools and community leadership (Riley and Louis 2005). We argued that while the leadership implications of aligning schools and communities had been largely unexplored in the literature, communities – including poor communities – are full of untapped resources: the 'nous' that comes from organizing a fund-raising event for a distant disaster, the skills from running the junior football club, and these resources go well beyond the strong social relationships that emerge from sharing the care of children (see e.g., Bauch 2001). We outlined the challenges facing school leaders in taking on these new roles in the following terms:

> If they currently teach, manage school finances, coordinate professional development, and work with new governing boards, they are already pressed. Working to engage disparate community groups that may have resources to buttress the school's goals is very time consuming and may have little short-term payoff. The notion that school leaders have community responsibilities that go beyond educating students is so new that current school leaders have few role models or honed skills to help them begin these tasks.
>
> (Riley and Louis 2005, p. 23).

Leadership on the Front-line highlighted the pace, complexity and day-to-day challenges faced by headteachers in community contexts which are demanding and volatile. It raised questions about the capacity of British society (as other societies) to respond to the fast-changing ethnic, cultural and socio-economic complexities and pressures which characterize some inner city areas, and which have an impact on society as a whole. It provided stark examples of the types of community challenge that school leaders have to manage daily. Many leaders experience relentless social and community pressures, and often find themselves serving as the only visible interface between disempowered communities and a whole range of public institutions (Riley et al. 2005).

I visited a school in Belfast, immediately after the principal had been threatened with violence by an irate mother. The principal commented, 'she must have been having a bad hair day'. This sanguine response was not dismissive of the mother, or of the seriousness of what had just taken place. It was a recognition by the principal that she was one of the few authority figures in the immediate reach of someone struggling to cope on the boundaries of society. The threat of violence, while real, was not personal. School leaders, such as the Belfast principal, have to maintain their own view of what is right and fair, equitable and just, often in the face of the diametrically opposed viewpoints of children, parents and communities who came from a range of religious, ethnic, political and economic backgrounds.

As well as being aware of these pressures, I was also struck by the joys and rewards of the job and the ways in which, if school leaders work in partnership with staff, pupils and communities, they can help make a difference to the lives of children and young people. By adhering to their values, they could create the space for the voices of marginalized and disenfranchised to be heard.

I began to reflect that schools could create something very precious in a crowded world: namely a sharable space which brought communities together. The two questions which then emerged for me were:

- What did leaders need to do to create that space?

- What could help them move from understanding the context of the communities to making sense of the place which those communities inhabited?

Questions for discussion and reflection

1 In what ways is the community in which you work changing?

2 What does this mean for the lives of young people?

3 How can the school respond to these changes?

INTRODUCTION

Locality studies

A framework for learning

The three locality studies are in New York, London and South Africa's Eastern Cape. They are rooted in the perspectives of young people and school leaders and offer a focus on context and community. The aim is to offer educators insights that will enable them to look afresh at their own contexts. The studies raise questions about:

- What young people think and experience within their neighbourhood?
- Where do they feel safe?
- Where they and their families think they belong?

The New York and London studies pick up on issues discussed in Chapter 3 about displacement, movement and change in an urban context. In the Eastern Cape, the spectre of the city looms large. Although their geographical settings are rural, they are a part of huge urban hinterlands. There, urban hinterlands drive the hungry and the 'go-getter' away from their local communities to the city (even though 'A Place Called Home' may turn out to be a bed in an overcrowded hostel), largely stripping the community of its working generation.

In all three contexts, education is a way forward, a way out. Education is liberation, not only in the Eastern Cape but also elsewhere. Education can help transform poor communities. It can provide young people with options and choices. In all three contexts, if young people can find their way across the threshold of the school, leave behind what holds them back and embrace the opportunities of education, the world will unfold for them. In all three contexts, schools and their leaders matter. Schools can help transform lives. They can also be negligent of the lives they have in their care. There are elements of the stories which follow in these chapters that may shock you. These are the stories of abuse, violence and neglect. But these stories are only part of the picture. Some of these tales have good endings. While the lives of many of the young people we meet may be constrained by poverty, or limited economic means, there are also riches. There is love and warmth and caring. There is friendship. Many of these accounts demonstrate the spirit and openness of the young people themselves and their appreciation of what schools can offer them. What shines through is the hope of the young people, the aspirations of communities and the dedication and energy of school leaders at many levels of a school. These are the leaders who are prepared to go that extra mile for the children and young people in their charge.

School leaders face many difficult decisions in response to their 'reading' of the challenges in the communities they work with. In responding to these challenges, the school leaders we meet in the next three chapters have chosen various paths to take. These include:

- building and deepening connections with communities

- providing space within the life of the school for young people to voice their concerns about deeply felt, and often controversial issues

- challenging the power of the street by recognizing its lure and bringing street life into the school, so that young people can learn to develop a different response

- putting a distance between the school and the community and supporting young people in breaking the link

These leadership responses are finely nuanced. School leaders may adopt all, or a mixture of these options, depending on circumstances. The aspiration that the school leaders share is to make school a safe place where it is 'cool' to learn, and where learning can create self-reliance in young people.

In reading the accounts which follow, I would encourage you to reflect on your own responses as a leader to the circumstances which face you.

A framework for thinking

The structure used in the three locality studies for exploring the challenges of leadership is called *Taking the Leadership Pulse*. This framework is drawn from the *Leadership on the Front-line* project. I developed it as a way of identifying the four elements that influence school leaders' ability to manage the four realities of leadership: the physical reality, the social or political reality, the emotional reality and the spiritual reality (Riley 2008).

- The *physical reality* encompasses the built environment and what routinely happens within it. This includes the daily events that are part of school life, and the lives and experiences of children and young people. It also involves the day-to-day logistics of managing a school in a challenging environment, in which the physical conditions can be daunting as well as invigorating.

- The *social and political reality* is shaped by the social landscape of the school (the relationships among people) and also the reality of students' home lives which – in the areas we are examining here – typically include poverty, lack of stability or neighbourhood tensions. The *political reality is* generated, to a large degree, by the attitudes and decisions of politicians, at both national and local levels.

- The *emotional reality* is influenced by the physical and social conditions. Emotions can be intense in challenging schools – not only for staff but for students too. The leaders of schools in socially disadvantaged communities can experience exhaustion, frustration and anger.

- The *spiritual and ethical reality* is the belief that drives leaders at all levels in a school. For some, this reality is linked to religious faith, for others, to a strong commitment to social justice. This dimension is the rock that holds school leaders together in stormy times. It manifests itself as a drive to enable young people to gain a sense of who they are, where they are from and who they might become.

At the time the framework was developed, I suggested that through recognizing the four realities of leadership, school leaders could build a sense of wholeness. This sense of wholeness makes it possible for them to acknowledge the challenges and the joys: the children themselves, their liveliness and exuberance; the support of staff and senior teams; the pleasure in seeing a child or a member of staff enlivened by the experience of learning in new ways. It also made it more likely that they would be able to reconcile, what – on the face of it – appear to be irreconcilable views and beliefs, and strike a balance between the unremitting demands of the job and a sense of personal well-being. This balance and focus will contribute to rich educational gains for students, staff and communities – and for school leaders themselves.

In the following chapters on the United States, the United Kingdom and South Africa, I have used the framework in two ways. The first has been to explore how school leaders conceptualize their leadership and the second, to examine how they respond to their role in helping to create and sustain a 'place' for young people.

CHAPTER FOUR

What's in a neighbourhood? – Stories from Brooklyn, New York

What's in a neighbourhood – Cobble Hill?

Walk along Smith Street in Brooklyn, away from the bustling bargain stores of Fulton Mall, and you enter Cobble Hill's world of boutique shops and health food bars. Walk further West along Henry Street's genteel pavements and Brooklyn Heights beckons. A number of publicly funded schools are to be found among these pleasant streets: in the neighbourhood, but not of the neighbourhood.

One result of New York City's school choice system is that New Yorkers can elect to send their children to any public school within the city's boundaries. This does not mean that they will necessarily get their 'choice', but movement across the city is becoming the norm. The neighbourhood school still exists, but growing numbers of young people travel from their 'hoods' to neighbourhoods which are very different from the daily worlds they inhabit.

In this chapter, I offer stories which give a sense of the complexities of young people's lives: the ways in which their communities may be divided, or their lives caught up in experiences that would tax the most resilient adult. The context for this exploration is Brooklyn, one of New York's five boroughs: a culturally and ethnically diverse district with distinct neighbourhoods and a defined downtown area. This chapter is neither an overview of New York's complex school system, nor a critique of its policy agenda. It is a small window into the lives of some young people.

As I stand at an intersection in Cobble Hill and watch the young people from the public schools spill onto the pavement, I am struck by the differences in lives and experiences: between the worlds of this lively African-American and Hispanic student population and those of the affluent, predominantly white local community. The humour and energy of the young people is at odds with the tranquil streets. An affluent shopper pulls her shopping bags to herself and with a shrug scurries on. The boutique jeans shop I had passed earlier has already dropped the catch. Shoppers now enter with permission. Other shops had developed niche markets in response to the ban on electronic devices in New York's schools: *Store your cell here – $1/day.* Security staff – employees of New York City's Police Department – line the streets to the subways.

I begin to think about what I see and what it all means for schools. In a context in which young people are visitors to a neighbourhood of which they are not a part, two questions occur to me:

1   How can local school leaders know and understand young people's lives and experiences?

2   How can they enable young people to find their place in a world that is so complex and to feel 'safe' in a neighbourhood that is not theirs as well as in their own neighbourhoods?

My opportunity to explore these issues in this vast and complex city arose through the goodwill of some of New York's principals and with the agreement of the New York State Education Department. During my time in New York, I visited seven schools, five of these in Brooklyn. To strengthen my exploration of place, I have chosen to focus on the Brooklyn schools. The schools are located in three particular neighbourhoods: broadly speaking, around Cobble Hill, Williamsburg and Brooklyn Bridge. Before exploring my questions, I want to add something about the other two Brooklyn localities and to explore the policy context of New York and its school system.

What's in a neighbourhood? Williamsburg

I'm sitting in a Pan-Asian organic vegan restaurant, ten minutes walk away from East Middle School which serves a predominantly Hispanic community. Williamsburg also has a large Hasidic Jewish population, but the two communities live separate lives. The street they share is called Division Avenue.

The restaurant is in an up and coming part of Williamsburg which seems a world apart from the neighbourhood surrounding East School. The school's Hispanic neighbourhood consists of blocks of flats (apartment buildings) and small shops selling *zapatos* (shoes) or *churros* (fried dough). Strolling along the streets, I realize that I have never seen so many shops and services for dogs in one area: dog grooming parlours, dog accessory shops, grocers selling 'galettas de perro', etc. I stop to admire a community garden, which takes pride of place: a place for neighbours to meet, to grow their vegetables, to enjoy the space and the light.

East School's Hispanic communities (from the Dominican Republic, Puerto Rico and Ecuador) now face the prospect of moving from an area where their families have been established for some time to the far reaches of New York State. Only 6 months earlier, those families could have rented a two-bedroom apartment for $500 a month, but the forward march of gentrification has driven rentals for a refurbished one-bedroom apartment up to $1,500 a month.

Finding and maintaining a place in the city is hard not only for the poor and the dispossessed, as discussed in Chapter 2, but also for the low-wage earner, particularly at a time of economic recession and in an area of urban transformation. Prospects for the long-established communities are not good. Hispanic families who have avoided the stigma of living in city 'projects' could find they are forced to take refuge there. Economic forces and the influx of more affluent populations may leave them with little or no choice about where to live.

The changes being experienced in the neighbourhood around East School mirror those elsewhere in New York. Neighbourhoods change. Sometimes the changes are rapid, as in Williamsburg, and at other times more evolutionary. Change is visible everywhere in Williamsburg. It's in the neighbourhood around East School and it's in the composition of the school's student body. A school that was 99 per cent Hispanic now has a growing number of African-American students, drawn there by the closure of schools in the project areas of Harlem, as well as by the increase in school choice brought about by *Mayor Bloomberg's education reforms*. The school's academic profile is also changing, as students (particularly the more academically able) are increasingly drawn to Charter Schools. All of these issues provoke my third Brooklyn-related question about leadership in this place:

3 What is the school's role when the locality is changing and the certainties that communities have had about place are fast disappearing?

What's in a neighbourhood? Brooklyn Bridge

Downtown School is close to the Brooklyn Bridge, located in a world of highways, underpasses and overpasses. Walk a mile or so to the West and you can find some of Brooklyn's most notable eateries: Grimaldi's Pizzeria with its renowned charcoal kilns, the River Cafe with its breathtaking views over the East River. There is Dumbo, an acronym for Down Under the Manhattan Bridge Overpass. It is New York's 90th historic district and an area of art galleries and community events. There is the Promenade at Brooklyn Heights whose breathtaking views over Manhattan sadly provided a global audience with some of the most powerful images of the collapse of the Twin Towers.

The area around Downtown school is a mixed bag: Brooklyn's financial district, derelict warehouses, desirable one-bedroom apartments, with their security-enhanced doors, on sale to the new urban élite at $1,550,000 and so forth. New York's extensive subway system enables young people to travel to the school from many parts of the city. The school was originally an alternative school for students who failed high school. Now as Smith Street Schools 1, 2 and 3, it has its specialist focus.

It takes me some time to find the school through the maze of one-way systems. Downtown is housed on the top two floors of an empty warehouse. It is one of the bleakest school buildings that I have ever visited: metal shutters across the windows, an air of quiet dilapidation. When I finally find the right entrance into the building, I am greeted by a pleasant security officer who tells me that the lift isn't working – a regular occurrence. There is no welcome to the world of the school, no celebration of the achievements of its young people. The janitor takes me into the next-door building, where the lift is working and from which I will be able to gain access to the school. I am puzzled how the school comes to be in such a desolate location. This gives me one more question to think about and leads me to reflect on the contextual issues about New York, its school system and its reform agenda (see box).

4   How can school leaders create a sense of place for young people in buildings that are so unwelcoming?

New York

New York is a global city, significant for its economic, cultural and political status (Sassen 1991). With the presence of the United Nations, it is the home of international diplomacy. Its role as a major international transport and access hub strengthens its international status. With a population of over 8 million, New York is the largest city in the United States and the seventh largest in the world. Some 800 languages are spoken in its five boroughs: the Bronx, Brooklyn, Manhattan, Queens and Staten Island. In 2010, the city's population was 33 per cent white (non-Hispanic), 23 per cent black (non-Hispanic) and 13 per cent Asian (the fastest growing group). Hispanics of any race represent 29 per cent of the population. The 2010 census data also confirmed the high level of housing segregation in the city.

New York's school system

The New York State Education Department serves about 1.1 million students, employs over 36,000 people and has an annual budget of $23 billion. It is the largest public school system in the world.

In 2002, billionaire Michael Bloomberg took over as Mayor, with a specific remit to overhaul the school system. Bloomberg introduced a series of reforms, under the umbrella title *Children First*, which focused on competition, choice, accountability and standards, with a strong emphasis on test results. As part of the overhaul of the NYS system, schools labelled as unsuccessful were closed: a number of these had been located in socially and economically deprived areas. The emphasis on choice and smaller schools has led to a significant increase in the number of schools, from 1,200 to the current figure of 1,700.

Opinion is divided about the success of these reforms. In a 2012 speech to the US Conference of Mayors, *Bloomberg reported on the* growth and development of New York City's educational reforms in the following terms:

> We've opened 139 new charter schools in our city, and we've created more than 500 new small schools, non-charters, but ones that give parents of kids top-quality options. Parents and students both deserve that. And school choice is an important way to hold schools accountable for success because when people vote with their feet you know that it's real and it's pretty obvious which direction they are going.
>
> (Usmayors 2012)

However, a *New York Times* survey in 2010 reported that 6 in 10 New Yorkers were dissatisfied with the quality of the city's public schools and did not believe that Bloomberg's reforms had improved the situation (*New York Times* 2010). In 2011, the National Assessment of Educational Progress (NAEP) published its report on the performance of children across the United States. Known as the 'Nation's Report Card', NAEP is a Federal test which compares the progress of fourth and eighth-graders (age 9–10 and 13–14) in 21 large cities. The Report indicated weaknesses in the New York system, an issue which New York journalist Sol Stern took up:

> The disappointing NAEP performance of . . . eighth-graders is particularly significant for our city's future. We might usefully

think of this cohort of about 80,000 students as 'Bloomberg's children.' That's because they started out in kindergarten in September 2002, just two months after the state legislature voted to give Mayor Bloomberg *total control* of the schools. The mayor promised that new accountability measures would reform the previously 'dysfunctional' and 'sclerotic' school system and help newly entering students to improve their academic performance and achieve higher graduation rates.

(Stern 2011)

Funding has been another area of controversy. Critics claimed that schools which had made major improvements in raising attainment lost their funding because they could not sustain an upward trajectory. Meanwhile, funding shifted to schools whose achievements were less, but more timely. Diane Ravitch, a critic of liberal school reforms and an assistant secretary of education in the first Bush administration, has been one of these critics. Ravitch has argued that the reforms she has advocated on testing, accountability, choice and markets have been 'hijacked' by the 'privatizers', particularly the Charter School movement. With backing from government and a range of foundations, these schools were drawing the best students and most committed parents away from the public and parochial (faith-based) school systems (Ravitch 2010).

Leading in Brooklyn

Politics, location and mobility are all ingredients in the New York leadership of place story. There are similarities and differences in the ways that these stories play out in the five Brooklyn schools. The three schools Cobble Hill schools are near each other: two are in the same building, and the third is no more than 100 yards away. Thus, the locality description at the beginning of the chapter is relevant to all three. I have called these schools Smith Street 1, 2 and 3. Smith Street 1 is a 6–12th grade school with more than

600 students and Smith Street 2 has just over 500 students. Smith Street 3 is a high school (grades 9–12) serving 750 students. Each school has its specialized curriculum focus and distinctive student population, but broadly speaking, the student population in each is predominantly African-American, Hispanic and Yemeni. Most of the students attending the three schools are not from the immediate neighbourhood, although a number live within walking distance.

Williamsburg's East School has a predominantly Hispanic student population although, as mentioned, it now recruits a growing number of African-American students. Previously a High School, it has been restructured into a smaller middle school with 420 students, as part of New York's school reforms. Each year group has a different focus: performing arts, journalism, maths and science.

Downtown offers a full academic curriculum to its 230 predominantly African-American students (65 per cent of the student body); a further 30 per cent is Hispanic and 5 per cent Asian. The school had a programme of legal studies which had been expanded to include Humanities. Most of the students travel some distance from housing projects, priority social housing and other poorer areas to attend the school.

The physical reality

The physical realities of leadership in the Cobble Hill schools are shaped by the contrasts between the lives of the young people attending them: between street life and school life, between their home neighbourhoods and the neighbourhoods they live in and those they go to school in. Michael, Principal of Smith Street School 1 described the area around the school as follows:

> We're in Cobble Hill, which is an affluent area. It's not a normal part of Brooklyn. A lot of times the neighbours look with distain at the kids. They're interlopers in a rich neighbourhood. A lot of our kids come from the projects (public housing). The nearest is four blocks away.

The affluent neighbourhood around Cobble Street was a world away from the projects and from the pressures that characterized the lives of many students and their families:

What you see for our kids are the profound effects of poverty. There's real poverty, kids have no shoes, no jackets . . . When I first came here the level of anger from parents was a shock to me. There are cases where there are sexual issues for kids – molestation. In any urban environment you'll find it.

For Maria, Principal of Smith Street School 3, the pervasiveness of poverty created a backdrop of struggle for her pupils:

> We have kids who are the breadwinners in their families. Some don't have their own beds at home. They're living in foster homes, living in homeless shelters. There are lots of grandparents looking after kids. There are issues about drugs. For the four years they are here, we become the home and the family.
>
> We have kids from all over Brooklyn. It's a Title 1 school; over 60 per cent are below the poverty line. Some are very needy and transient. Some come here with a commute of over one hour.

Bob, the principal of Smith Street School 2, spoke in a similar vein of the weight of socio-economic pressures on the young people living in housing projects. 'Society's issues are overwhelming. I feel we're fighting a fight that is larger than us'. Poverty, alcohol and substance abuse all had an impact on their ability to be successful. Young people in all three schools had parents who were working and who had strong cultural connections with their roots, for example, Hispanic or Yemini. Many had two jobs to support their families, because money was hard to come by. Given these pressures, some found it difficult to be sufficiently involved in the lives of their children. It was important, Bob argued, not to judge them.

> When you find yourself thinking 'you're too young to be having so many kids', you have to judge your own cultural expectations . . . You have to be careful not to fall into that trap. When you see a kid misbehaving and at risk and you call in a parent and she can't give her attention . . . you feel like saying to mom . . . 'That's not the way to support good behaviour'. . . . You have to go deep into the well of your compassion.

Safety was a daily concern for the principals. Michael from Smith Street I had appointed a security officer to 'walk the halls'. All three Cobble Hill principals felt they had to be constantly vigilant. Michael explained this as follows:

> Weapons are not a problem in the school but the Prom celebration was a military operation for the safety of our students. . . . Sometimes I've had to bring in our own security to protect staff.
>   There is a level of violence and gang mentality. They're either involved in gangs or want to be part of clique of fake gangsters. You get lots of jumpings on the way home . . . The girls are vicious and sometimes much worse than the boys. 70 per cent of the fights involve females. The boys seem docile in comparison.

Critical challenges for Lena at East School in Williamsburg were catering for the English as a second language (ESL) needs of the predominantly bilingual student population and responding to the changing ethnic composition of the school. The arrival of a cohort of African-American students into a culturally homogeneous Hispanic school community had created difficulties. She explained it as follows:

> We have the new students, some from the projects, many with baggage, coming into a predominantly Hispanic school. We've seen an increase in racial conflict and some real challenges. We had a fight down in the cafeteria between two African-American and two Spanish females. It was real Thelma and Louise stuff. The safety agent had to separate them.
>   It all sprang up from texting and Facebook. The African-American students take the line 'I'm going to get you before you get me.' And the Hispanic students are not going to stay quiet. Thankfully there were only a few supporters. I said 'We're not going to have West Side story here'. Now I've put out an edict: 'No cell phones'.

Downtown School had to meet the pressing needs of a student population characterized by high levels of poverty (85 per cent + receiving free or reduced-price lunches); and a myriad of family problems. 'School becomes the only stable place they know', Carla commented, 'We have to hold them responsible for what they do and also match their emotional needs'.

The social and political reality

As elsewhere in New York, the social and political reality of leadership in Brooklyn is shaped by the changing policy environment as well as by socio-economic conditions. The challenge for the principals was to keep the young people engaged and focused. Attendance was an immediate and ongoing problem as Michael commented:

> I'm aiming for 95 per cent. Some come for a few dates to get a free metro card. Some come for one or two key dates to keep the welfare cheques coming in for mom and dad. We've added lots of clubs and activities to encourage them to come in and we're paying teachers to do that. It's unusual.

Student recruitment was another challenge. Schools that couldn't raise their numbers faced competition from Charter Schools. All of the principals were concerned about Charter Schools, particularly the way they recruited their students. Lena from East School in Williamsburg described the process in the following terms:

> The Charter Schools have a significant impact on us. They're siphoning off our strongest students. They have access to the names and addresses of public schools, they solicit parents, they send letters in which they say 'you have been selected'. . . .

The other four principals echoed these worries. In the context of an increase in the number of schools in Brooklyn, Carla was concerned that 'The Mayor has a mind set about opening more schools' without acknowledging the consequences for neighbouring schools, such as Downtown. Despite the school's success on a range of criteria, it had lost 10 per cent of its budget as numbers had fallen. As a result, key projects which had had demonstrable positive effect on students had been forced to close.

Principals expressed a range of other policy concerns such as:

● 'The Board needs to focus on middle schools'.

● Policies were 'top down' and 'coming too fast' – even though some polices, such as on teacher evaluation which focused on teacher's performance, could be positive.

- 'No time to process anything. You just have to deliver'.

- admission' policies ('This year there were 10,000 kids who didn't get one of their 10 choices'.)

- student performance ('Many of our students are without internet access at home and they are competing across the system with other students who must be some of the most well-resourced in the world'.)

- security

The New York State Education Department has stringent policies aimed at preventing violence in schools. Dependent on the perceived level of threat, schools are designated as either 'impact' or 'non-impact' schools. An impact school has tougher security, including metal detectors at the entrance. Michael commented on the knife-edge decision-making needed to operate within this policy environment, 'No school wants to become an impact school. Parents don't want that'. He explained the dilemma in the following terms:

> Last year we had two infractions to do with violence. The 'big wigs' came down to see. . . . The Office of School Safety decides whether a school is an impact or non-impact school. It was a near miss for us. There are some real difficulties in how you report incidents, how you keep it at one level and from being seen as going to the next levels of incidents!

The emotional reality

For Michael, the political reality of managing this situation was also part of his emotional reality: and it challenged his emotional equilibrium. He went on to outline other examples of the tension in balancing the needs of individuals and the well-being of the school overall thus:

> Drugs can be an issue in the schools. The kids used to go out to lunch but I've stopped it because I'm worried about drugs. I know some students may be selling drugs. . . . The amount of marijuana that we seized from students is extraordinary.

But as a principal, we're caught out; we're walking a thin line. If the kids are suspended by the school they can be arrested. It's not easy. If the kids are caught in possession of drugs, they can't get any financial aid for college.
With one phone call, you can destroy a kid's future.
But another suspension. . . . Who does that help?

The emotional realities of leadership are powerful for all five principals, as they deal with students' family circumstances, staff performance or student behaviour. Attending to staffing matters could be very stressful, and principals had to get through trying encounters and negotiations by keeping their minds focused on the well-being of their students:

- When I came here, things weren't working for the kids. We've now got 12 new members of staff out of 40. They moved on own accord but with helpful counselling!! It wasn't easy.

- I brought in new staff and kept the acting principal as my assistant. It created a lot of trouble. He was pissing in the well!

- The previous Principal had been arrested. I had to pick up the pieces.

- I went into the classrooms and saw what went on. . . . I had some very difficult conversations.

- I had to face the challenges of union opposition to reforms.

There could be a mismatch between what teachers provided and what children needed, as Carla commented:

Staff want to teach their subject area, but they're teaching children with moods and feelings. They have to learn how to see them as individuals but still teach them. The kids come with so many needs and issues. School is socially dumped on. It's the only place they can get help. Some families are embarrassed by the extent of their poverty. Kid comes to school asking themselves, where am I going to sleep? Will I have food?
The only thing that will make a difference is getting them educated.

It could be frustrating to deal with pupils' destructive behaviour. Principals spoke of students 'who didn't fear God, man or beast', or who 'trashed everything in sight' – and yet, who 'could be likeable' when not in a rage. However, the deepest emotional toll sprang from bearing witness to the realities of life for some young people, as Carla from Downtown explained:

> There was a young woman who had been date raped. She was one month shy of being 18. I knew this had happened because she confided in a friend. I talked to the father and he asked 'Did she enjoy it?' We had our suspicions that they were sleeping together. He'd raised the girl to have no self-esteem. He was saying . . . I find nothing wrong taking my share of my daughter. I was so distraught and angry, I felt like punching him in the face. It's stayed with me. I have to remember, they're not my children.

The spiritual and ethical reality

In responding to these extremes, principals drew on their own deep-rooted spiritual and ethical realities. They were driven by personal beliefs and deeply rooted commitments to making a difference. These commitments were faith-based, or sprang from a well of belief in social justice and the liberating powers of education. Carla described herself as:

> A woman of faith . . . It's my centre my anchor . . . that enables me to come in here every day with a smile on my face. . . . This job gives me the chance to make a difference. . . .

Lena, who had been brought up in Barbados, said that making a difference was a passion for her. 'I've been privileged in my life . . . I can't fathom how some of the kids can have such nice dispositions, given what they have to put up with'. The rewards came from the young people themselves, as Michael explained:

> The kids keep you going . . . Just walking through the halls keeps me going and puts everything in perspective. One 6th grader said 'thank you for making the school better'.

Being and becoming a leader of this place

Bob had been drawn to his school because it was a place that needed to change to meet the needs of its young people.

I was attracted to this school because it was a failing middle school. I responded to that. When I walked into the building the kids were all over the halls. Nothing was happening. This place needed help. It was like walking into an overgrown garden. I liked the challenge. I liked I could walk home. It's right here in my community.

He lived locally and felt himself to be an integral part of the community. This is not an option for all principals or their staff and they can respond to place in a number of ways. One option is to develop the relationship between the school and the local community, ensuring that the school becomes a place of safety and opportunity, and a place that understands and values what communities have to offer. This is Bob's approach:

I just want to create a place that kids can feel safe to be who they are. That's a learning environment of rapport, respect, competence, and love. Kids can smell it. They know when it is there and when it's not.

Kids have to have a sense that you know where they are coming from, that you respect and acknowledge their community. If you seem a total outsider who has no respect for their lives, families and culture, you have no place here and they have no place. You have to be authentic. Kids are intuitive and perceptive.

Bob saw his role as being localized in that space. His absolute commitment was to the children and young people in the school:

I only bring people here who love kids of other cultures. But sometimes it's hard to sniff that out on interview. . . . I connect to the kids . . . I live seven blocks away, they see me in the swimming pool and in supermarkets, markets they shop in. I walk to work. That's how I stay connected. I would like to do more home visits. One home visits goes a long way.

Staff don't necessarily understand the kids' lives . . . Their own experience is likely to be more middle class. They don't know about sharing a bedroom with siblings, waiting 40 min to shower, not knowing when you are going to eat again. A lot of teachers have less adult responsibilities than our students. They're middle class college kids full of idealism . . . but they may go in the wrong direction. They are overcome by fatigue and the behaviour of the kids.

From this standpoint, the challenge of leadership of place is about trying to make school one of the few places where young people want to be: a place that is safe; a place where it is 'cool' to learn; a place that is enriching. However, creating these opportunities can be an isolating and intense experience. It requires principals to 'be at the helm – watching out for security'; to be focused on how to motivate teachers and how to act on their knowledge about what is 'brewing' in the neighbourhood. All of this demands personal sacrifices. 'I never get home in time to bath the baby' Michael commented.

A second (and interrelated) leadership option is to focus on the role of the school in developing self-reliance in the students in ways that will prepare them to be socially conscious. This, in Bob's view, was the first step towards enabling them to become 'citizens of the world'. For Bob, leadership of place was about being a 'tribal leader', strengthening the school as a social unit which is bigger than a group but smaller than society.

The challenges of leadership of place for Lena at East School stem from two sets of changes which are affecting the relatively homogenous Hispanic community. The first set of changes look set to divide and disperse the local community. There are strong expressions of anger in local papers, and there is a growing lobby to defend the local community and its achievements, such as a gardening project that involves young people from the school. The established community feel they are being pushed out. And they are. They are losing their place. Economic forces, urban regeneration and the arrival of the as yet childless urban elite, will transform the locality. While there will be some benefits to the local community, there will also be many down sides. Within the school itself, there are changes in the composition of the student population. Charter Schools are drawing away some of the most academically able.

African-American students from New York's projects have arrived with their own cultural characteristics as well as with their need to find a place for themselves.

Changes in the ethnic and social composition of a locality or a school can have significant consequences, as discussed in Chapter 2, In East School in Brooklyn, young women from the school's growing African-American community fight for the space and territory held by their more established Hispanic 'sisters'. Facebook and Twitter become vehicles for building up fears, establishing new rivalries, consolidating opposition. A reprise of *West Side Story* is fast in the making: my space, my culture, my identity.

School leaders need to understand the importance of these cultural issues, and the clashes which can emerge, as communities, particularly poor communities, fight to establish their place in the city. One of Lena's key strategies, particularly as an African-American woman, has been to recognize the importance of culture to the established local community. She used her influence to persuade the School District to bring in a new, and in her view excellent, Vice-Principal who was male and Hispanic.

> The demographics matter. It was about showing the community that we took them seriously. He's very good. There was a kick back from the community when I came in.

For Lena, recognizing the cultural capital in the community – the strength and importance of local networks, community groups and initiatives – has also been critical. Equally important has been acknowledging the emotional dissonance felt by the young Hispanic members of the school community as 'outsiders' moved in, and the reactions and alienation of those African-American 'outsiders'. Her first step was to enforce a strong disciplinary code of behaviour. The second was to begin to challenge the attitudes and perceptions of both groups. Her way in was to focus on the impact of cyber bullying. She invited Tina Meier to come and talk about the death of her daughter Megan.

Megan Taylor Meier from Missouri committed suicide in 2006, shortly before her fourteenth birthday. Her death was linked to cyber-bullying through the social networking website MySpace (Megan Meier Foundation 2011). Lena described the powerful impact of Tina Meier's talk on the school's young audience. It provided a common language for students from both communities (Hispanic and African-American) to talk about bullying and cyber bullying and its impact on their lives.

Carla at Downtown has to contend with a different set of issues. The students are not from the local area, so she cannot engage with the local community in the ways that are more open to Lena or Bob. For Carla, the only hope for the school's young people who came from deeply dysfunctional families was to create a degree of space between school and home. The tension for her was between preparing these students to take their place in society while at the same time counteracting some of their experiences of community life.

> The skills that kids use to survive living in the projects are not the ones they need to live their lives in the future. That aggressive persona, 'They disrespect me . . . Why are you looking at me?' won't help them. The skills they use to prevent themselves being victims are not the skills to be educated. They don't need to be disrespectful or harsh.

The school's role was to be their advocate, to provide a safe environment, to have conversations with young people about their situation, helping them recognize, for example, that if their parents had been able to get their children out of poverty they would have done so. It was now up to the young people themselves.

> Lots of kids don't have much hope for themselves. They don't see themselves as doing very much. They need to figure out their dreams. What they can do with their lives, how they can get through High School. They have to figure out they can go to College. They have to figure out how to get out of New York. They can get a financial aid package for New York State.
>
> You come to realise that you need to help them, move them out of their neighbourhood. They are less successful if they stay at home. There are a lot who are not able to survive their environments. Living in their projects, neighbourhoods, the gangs are always present. The violent behaviour is always there. You have to help them think outside the box.

At a profound level, the school's role was to create a belief in the young people that there were possibilities, and to enable them to find their place in the world. For Carla, this could be achieved in one of two ways. The first approach was to break the cycle. She had to recognize that for some, this meant breaking the link with home, going to college away from home and finding their place in the world at some distance from their homes. She was keen to identify where and when the school could intervene.

> We had a girl whose stepmother would beat her, a real Cinderella story of abuse and trauma. The family kept saying 'what's so special about her?' We got her a scholarship and she went away to College and the College banned the family from visiting. There was another girl who had been raped. She told me she was going home to ram a knife up her throat. I couldn't let her leave, I semi-adopted her. She used to stay with me in the evenings until 8pm or so.

The second approach was to build bridges with young people that acknowledged the realities of their lives and offered strategies for moving ahead. The school recognized that many issues were different for girls than for boys. Girls faced the dangers of early pregnancy and a high dropout rate from college. Carla observed:

> How do we build their self-esteem and help them realise that when a guy says 'you're pretty', they don't have to spread your legs? . . . Being a principal, I've learned so much about sex . . . It's about having conversations with them about respect and about not being an object. It's about respecting their privacy and helping them draw on the resources outside school and the support that is there in their community. Many girls are in melt down. They've been raped or molested, or they've lost their parents, in some way. There's abandonment issues.

An issue for boys was low graduation rates; at one time only 1 in 5 boys graduated from the school. Many lacked basic skills, 'We realized that the boys didn't read, so they couldn't write'. The school created single sex reading classes for their male, predominantly African-American, students. Graduation rates for boys and girls are now the same. Both have risen substantially.

The school also developed a successful programme for young men called *Rights of Passage*, which brought in adults from the community to work with students. The programme recognized the lure of the streets:

We brought in a gang leader who had been in a Federal prison for ten years. He had currency with the kids. He could talk their language. The programme enabled them to drop their facade. What they learned from that programme was impossible to get on paper. He monitored their behaviour. They talked about how to deal with the gangs.

The programme allowed the students to raise issues about their lives which were not usually discussed in schools. It gave them 'a certain voice' to discuss these issues in a safe environment. The school has now lost funding for this programme.

My place: How young people see it

Towards the end of my discussion with the principal of Downtown school, a young Hispanic man was shown into her office. Apologizing for the interruption, Carla explained with pride that Antonio had come to pick up his High School Diploma. Carla asked him whether he might like to tell me something of his story. He did. He was off to junior college, and his pleasure at this achievement was palpable. He told me that his parents had thrown him out of his home and that the school had helped him to find a hostel – a safe and supportive place – where he had lived for the last two years. With the school's help, he had improved his basic skills, particularly in English, and developed his talents as an artist. Through the *Rights of Passage* programme he had been given a mentor who had helped him find his way. He was shocked to learn that the programme was ending. 'But for this school', he said, 'I would have been just another person hanging around on the streets'.

It is hard for those carrying out any type of system reform to appreciate the casualties that inevitably result from change. Reformers don't mean to close opportunities for future 'Antonios'; indeed the reverse is probably true. However, perceptions and realities may differ. And as has been discussed earlier in the chapter, perceptions are divided about the impact of New York's reforms.

In 2010, students from two schools in the borough of Queens – Jamaica High and Queens Collegiate – wrote a play entitled 'Declassified: Struggle for Existence (We Used to Eat Lunch Together)'.

It focuses on the impact of New York's school reforms from the standpoint of a group who thought that they were at the bottom of the pile and were losing out: losing their place and space in the city. The play was inspired by a blog from Jamaica High School teacher Marc Epstein, who chronicled a tale of Academic Apartheid. He argued that the decision to close Jamaica High (along with dozens of other schools) was based on faulty data and assumptions (Strauss 2010, 2011). The students' script drew on Antigone by Sophocles, as well as Seamus Heaney's version of *Antigone, The Burial at Thebes,* which centred on the conflicts between individual freedom and the imposition of restrictions by the state. *The Burial at Thebes* was a hard-hitting critique of the foreign policies of the 2004 Bush administration.

Antigone's punishment for defying the king of Thebes, Creon, is to be walled up in a cave. The Antigone of the students' play is suspended from school for leading a campaign of opposition to the closures. The play was banned and never performed. Nevertheless, it offers one set of views from the ground about the impact of the reforms on one group of students. The following extracts are from the students' text of the play. The play begins with two different accounts of a school day from the perspectives of two sisters, Antigone and Ismene: the former in a school which is under threat and the latter in a newly opened school:

Declassified: Struggle for Existence (We Used to Eat Lunch Together)

Extracts Scene I:

The two sisters *Antigone and Ismene come home from neighbouring schools.*

Mom: Hi Antigone. How was school?
Antigone: I don't want to talk about it.
Mom: Come on, it can't be that bad.
Antigone: There were 42 kids in my math class. There wasn't even a place to sit. Plus we don't have enough textbooks to go around. It's that bad.

Ismene enters

Mom: Hi sweetheart. How was your day?

Ismene: Mom, we have laptops. Can you believe it? I mean we can't take them home with us, but still . . .

Mom: So it was a good day?

Ismene: Besides the fact that now I have all these textbooks I have to lug around. Oh, and I need you to sign this paper. We are going on a field trip to D.C. next month.

Antigone: It's not fair. These new schools are getting all the attention. It's like we've been left out for the birds to feed on . . .

Scene II focuses on the local TV news, drawing on a New York Times article from 28 October 2010.

Extracts Scene II

TV: The New York City Department of Education said Thursday that up to 47 schools could be closed for poor performance, a huge increase from previous years if all remain on the chopping block. The schools on the list include John Dewey High School in Brooklyn and Jamaica High School in Queens.

TV: In the eight years since Mayor Michael R. Bloomberg has used school closings as a cornerstone of his school reform strategy, 91 schools have been shuttered and replaced with new schools. Nineteen of the schools were to close last year, but won temporary reprieves because of a lawsuit brought by the teachers' union and the National Association for the Advancement of Coloured People. The schools face a potential 'phase-out,' a process in which the school stops accepting students and loses one grade per year until it ceases to exist. Simultaneously, new schools open in the building.

Antigone: *(To Ismene)* That's where your school came from.

. . . .

Newscast ends. Antigone clicks off the TV.

As the play goes on, opposition to the closings mounts, with Antigone playing a key role.

Extracts Scene VII:

Mom is sitting at the table. She is tired from work. Antigone comes home.

Antigone: I can't believe this, Ismene and I had this whole protest planned. It was gonna be big. But now this! (*Holds up a letter*)

Mom: Antigone, Slow down! What's this all about?

Antigone: Ok, So the city decides it wants to close down Jamaica High School, right?! And I'm like no you don't! We're gonna fight this! So I start to talk to people, make posters. Some teachers, you know, they're in the fight, getting petitions signed and all that. Then just as it's heating up I get suspended.

Mom: Wait a minute. How come I didn't know about this?

Antigone: Please mom, just let me finish. Anyway, we get suspended for hanging posters where I'm not supposed to.

Mom: We got suspended?

Antigone: Yeah, well Ismene too. But that's a long story. She didn't really do it.

Mom: Ismene got suspended!?

Antigone: Mom! Will you please just listen!?

Mom: Fine. Go ahead.

Antigone: So while I'm suspended, I got some time on my hands, right? So I start thinking, what if we get all the students together, including the students from the new schools that are supposed to be like our competition . . . and all of us together march from the school to the Chancellor's office to say no to closing Jamaica High School.

She hands Mom the letter, who reads it aloud.

Mom: Dear Parents and Students, this letter is to inform you that the New York City Department of Education has decided to 'phase out' Jamaica High School. Beginning Fall of 2011, no incoming students will be admitted and the school will close by 2014.

Antigone: Word has come down from Creon. There's to be no rest, No mourning, and the corpse is to be publicly dishonoured.

Mom: Antigone, don't take it so hard. I mean, is the decision final?

Antigone: It sounds pretty final to me. . . . It just seems like we're fighting against the odds, just to survive, just for existence.

Mom: Listen to me Antigone, those are the fights worth fighting, the ones against the odds. I'm proud of you. You may be young, but it's the rightness that matters, not the age. I say keep fighting.

Antigone: Really? And you're not upset that I got suspended?
Mom: Come here. . . .

Mom gives Antigone a hug
Lights fade. Projections of past Jamaica High School protests.

The opportunity for me to talk with young people about their lives and experiences was limited to Smith Street School 1. The young people told me about their neighbourhood of high-rise flats (apartment buildings). This is what they loved about the area:

> Pizzas and my friends
> 　Baseball time and trying out.

And about their school:

> The teachers are nice in this school.
> 　I chose this school because they are all people from different religions and they get along.

While many were happy with their families, there was a consistent pattern in what made them unhappy in their lives outside school:

> In my house I am so happy here because I love it. But if there be shootings I'm so sad (Illustration 4.1).

ILLUSTRATION 4.1

> Sometimes you hear the police and helicopters. It's bad stuff when you hear the police alarm.
>
> It's not a good neighbourhood. The cops are searching around. Sometimes I hear gun shots. But I don't care. What matters is what is on the inside.

When I asked one young person, Dixon, to write about his neighbourhood, the good and the bad, he eyed me with disbelief. 'You want to know about my "hood"'? he asked. 'Yes', I replied. 'I want to know about your "hood" so that I can help your principal and other principals do a better job'. He asked again, 'You really want to know about my "hood?" No one has ever asked me about my "hood before."' And this is what he wrote in an account that vividly depicts the daily contrasts in his life (Illustration 4.2):

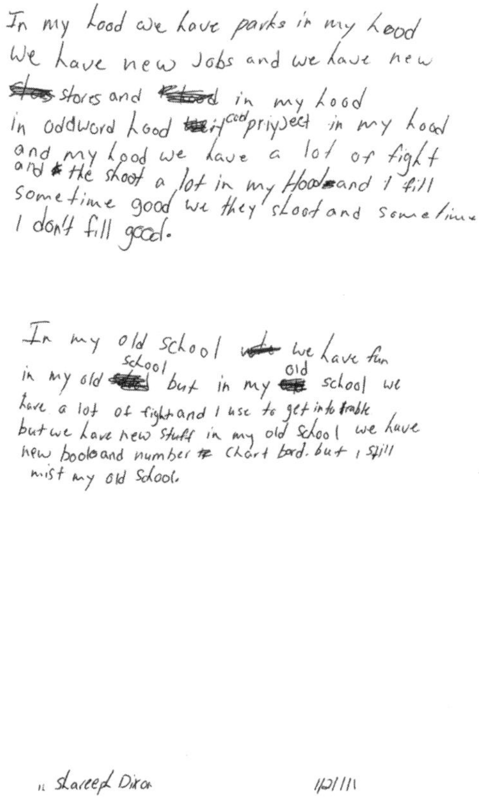
In my hood we have parks in my hood
We have new Jobs and we have new
stores and in my hood
in oddword hood cod priyject in my hood
and my hood we have a lot of fight
and the shoot a lot in my Hood and I fill
Sometime good we they shoot and Sometime
I don't fill good.

In my old School we have fun
in my old School but in my old School we
have a lot of fight and I use to get into trable
but we have new Stuff in my old School we have
new book and number chart bord. but I still
mist my old School.

Shareef Dixon 1/21/11

ILLUSTRATION 4.2

Michael told me later that Dixon lived in one of the projects. He had never seen him write so much before.

Some leadership learning points – Chapter 4

Given below are the five Leadership Learning Points from the chapter:

- Schools need to work closely with their communities but their responses must be finely nuanced. One leadership response is to become an integral member of the local community. However, this is not always an option.

- Where schools are at a distance from the homes of young people it can be difficult to engage with the local community. Young people can become the bridge that connects schools and communities.

- Leadership of place is exercised at many levels within a school. Teachers need to be good practitioners and enthusiastic about their areas of expertize. As leaders of place, knowing the circumstances and places where young people come from will make them even better teachers.

- In some communities, where families are deeply dysfunctional, schools may need to work with young people to help them put space between themselves and their families.

- School leaders need to understand cultural issues within the local communities, such as why and how clashes can emerge when communities, particularly poor communities, fight to establish their place in the city.

1 Which of these five points is closest to your own experience?

2 Is there a point you disagree with?

3 If so why?

CHAPTER FIVE

What's in this global city for me? – Stories from London's East End

What's this place?

On a grey winter's day I revisit London's East End. I want to see the area afresh, think about the ebb and flow and return to the neighbourhoods surrounding some of the schools I have worked with. I drive south through Waltham Forest, a borough of contrasts, past Epping Forest's 6,000 acres and the flood plains of the Lea Valley. This was an old dividing line for London; noxious industries were housed in the north away from the central city area. I reach the East End's northern outpost which is the tail end of the Borough and its poorest area.

The road ahead of me has been cordoned off by the police. There has been an 'incident'. I drive through the 'in-between' spaces of East London where the economic tide seems to have gone out. I stop at a corner and look at the three shops: a 'bookies' (betting office), a watchmaker and a pawnbroker. It is the world of '£1' shops. I pass the 'Immigrants' Legal Advisory Centre' in Hackney. Further south is Clapton Pond – a hint of gentrification – and then Tower Hamlets, the heart of the East End. I cross the Commercial Road in Whitechapel, home to the rag trade and strangely quiet on a Saturday, in contrast to the busy Saturday Asian market behind it. Five minutes later, I am at Tower Bridge, which is buzzing with tourists.

I meander my way back through Tower Hamlets to the Isle of Dogs, its shape familiar to TV fans of East Enders. I am struck yet again by the ways in which different worlds can exist in close proximity and yet rarely, if ever, intersect. I pass one of the schools I have worked with, which is close to the affluent banking and financial district of Canary Wharf. A student had illustrated this intersection of contrasting lives in a striking image: Illustration 5.1. The students are waiting at the bus stop. The bus – and its cache of white-collar office workers, senior hedge fund managers and private equity bosses – fails to stop for them. The grown-ups pass them by and the young people are left waiting. They continue to inhabit a different, and frustrating, world.

I am reminded of the intersection at Cobble Hill where I watched students pour out onto the pavement. Both Brooklyn and the East End of London are places of contrast. Poverty and gentrification sit cheek by jowl.

ILLUSTRATION 5.1

EAST END

Mention 'London's East End' and you conjure up many different images. As one of the cheapest areas of the city to settle in, it has been home to many generations of the struggling poor. To some, the East End epitomizes the stoicism and resilience of the British. Nazi propagandist Lord Haw-Haw, understanding the importance of the East End to the British psyche, proclaimed in a wartime broadcast:

> The Luftwaffe will smash Stepney. I know the East End! Those dirty Jews and Cockneys will run like rabbits into their holes.
>
> (Sheridan 2001)

The East End personifies the working-class spirit of the Pearly Kings and Queens, with their long-standing traditions of raising money for London's poor. The East End has its place in the annals of crime: Jack the Ripper and the Kray twins are a few of its famous villains. The River Thames provides one boundary for the East End, symbolizing adventure, travel and distant lands. The river's development is linked to the rise of Britain as a maritime nation. Whaling vessels set out for distant seas and merchant craft sailed to distant shores, setting their chronometers by Greenwich Mean Time (GMT), as they headed east towards the Thames Estuary. The mysteries of those journeys have echoed down the years, found in the songs children still sing today in schools in Greenwich:

> My ship sails to China with a cargo of tea, all laden with presents for you and for me. They gave me a fan; just imagine my bliss, when I found myself fanning like this . . . like this . . . like this.

The Thames has been the gateway into England for successive waves of immigrants: in the seventeenth century, it was the Huguenot refugees from France, and in the nineteenth century, it was the Irish and the Ashkenazi Jews from Eastern Europe. Now, at the beginning of the twenty-first century, London's Docks have declined, and the Thames is for tourist launches rather than for cargo boats. The East End has seen the ebb and flow of many cultures. There is a building on Brick Lane which has been an Anglican Church, a Methodist Chapel and a Synagogue. It is now a Mosque.

The East End was the focus of the early social reformers (R. H. Tawney, Clement Attlee and William Beveridge) who campaigned to change London's slum conditions in the late nineteenth and early twentieth centuries. Its radical history includes the Match Girls' strike of 1888, during which some 1,400 women and girls walked out of the Bryant and May factory in a fight against 14-hour work days, poor pay, excessive fines and the health risks associated with working with phosphorus, especially the debilitating condition 'Phossy Jaw'. At the turn of the twentieth century, the East End's radicalism contributed to the formation of the Labour Party, and Emmeline Pankhurst based her campaign for women's votes in the area. Sylvia Pankhurst set up the East London Federation of Suffragettes at a baker's shop in Bow.

The East End has witnessed collisions between opposing ideologies, and between impoverished groups struggling to find a place for themselves in the city. At the turn of the twentieth century, East End locals clashed with Irish and Jewish immigrants seeking work in the docks. In 1936, Oswald Mosley and his 'Blackshirts' in the British Union of Fascists threatened to march through the East End's streets. Anti-fascist groups opposing this move came to blows with police in what came to be known as the *Battle of Cable Street*. In 1993, the British National Party won its first local council seat in Millwall on the Isle of Dogs, fighting on a 'Rights for Whites' platform and alleging that black families were being favoured in local housing initiatives (Copsey 2004, pp. 53–4).

The East End today remains a place of contradictions. New and wealthier inhabitants are moving into the area. Brick Lane, its fame boosted in 2003 by Monica Ali's eponymous book which portrayed the Bengali community, now finds its shops and cafes as popular with tourists as local people. The East End is becoming one of the new 'cool' places to visit in London.

Come to the East End and witness some of the most overcrowded housing in Britain. Come to the East End and hit the tourist trail.

- Pass Jamie Oliver's 'social' restaurant.

- Admire the work of young British artists in Hoxton Square's galleries.

- Hunt for a bargain in a real East London market.

- Tuck into pie and mash in a traditional East End caff.

- Drop in on a clown school.

- Browse the stalls at chic Spitalfields and funky Brick Lane.

(Urban Adventures 2012)

Street life and school life

I chose the East End as my London study because of the contrasts. It reflects the dynamism of London as a diverse global city capable of constant reinvention. As a loose geographical area, the East End includes the wealthy medieval City of London, England's business capital; Tower Hamlets (with the financial district of Canary Wharf and some of Britain's poorest areas) and parts of three neighbouring boroughs, Hackney, Newham and Waltham Forest (Palmer 1989).

Red Bank School is a co-educational comprehensive secondary school in Tower Hamlets. It has some 600 students and is located in an impoverished, high-density area. There are no visible play areas. The 20-storey block of flats (apartment building) around the corner, casts a deep shadow on the horizon. The neighbouring public housing estate is a maze of pathways overlooked by security cameras. There are signs of gentrification. What was once a parade of shops has now become the front rooms of the latest, more affluent, settlers. Dilapidated social housing has been restored. As I stand on a street corner looking at old and new, a young Asian man stops and asks me with a smile, 'Can I help?'

The Borough of Tower Hamlets has the highest proportion of children eligible for free school meals in England, nearly 1 in 2, compared with 3 in 20 nationally.[1] Its Bangladeshi households are three times more likely to be in poverty as Indian or White households (Poverty Profile 2009). The socio-economic challenges facing Red Bank are typical of those across the borough. The school itself mirrors the density of its surrounding area. Students are confined to a tightly packed building. The boundaries between the school and the outside world are permeable. The Fire Assembly Point is a street corner. As the bell rings at the end of the school day, Red Bank's young people tumble out onto the streets, very much like their peers in Brooklyn's Cobble Street, with one significant difference. These young people are of this neighbourhood. Mary, Red Bank's headteacher, describes the area which lies just outside her office window. She explains the differing expectations of her predominantly Bengali and white working-class students thus:

[This neighbourhood] in itself is probably the most deprived area in the country. Within that, I think there are different types of poverty and perhaps for our white, working-class community there's a poverty of aspiration, as much as anything else. Among our Bangladeshi population there's often whole families where they don't know anybody who's either been to higher education or had full-time employment. However, there are often significant amounts of money through a black economy, but with lots of people working within one household in low paid jobs.

Massive overcrowding and, I think, a complete difference between the two communities in the way that they perceive education. So that in the white working-class population, often the families have had a negative view of education themselves and they transpose that onto their children, and they see that education has done nothing for me, therefore my child doesn't particularly need it . . . . And perhaps they live in the past . . . the days when you could leave school on Friday and go to work on Monday.

The Bangladeshi families on the other hand, have a sense that education will somehow give them a way out of this. So there is a value for education, and there is a willingness to try and participate in the educational process. However, there is a lack of knowledge about how to do that and it's up to us to try and help them to understand the educational process. I think what often happens is, they've had very limited education themselves and what they have had would have been in a very different setting. So, sometimes the expectations are quite unrealistic.

Mary's description captures the evolution of the locality. It illustrates the tensions between established and new communities: differences of views, beliefs and perspectives.

It's a community in which, in the 10 years or so that I've been here, has undergone quite significant change. And 10 years ago the tensions were between the Bangladeshi community and the White and Afro-Caribbean community. . . . To a large degree that's changed. Although our school mirrors [the Borough] almost exactly in its ethnic make-up, so we're about 55 per cent Bangladeshi, 30 per cent English, Welsh, Scottish, Irish, 10 per cent Afro-Caribbean and the rest is a mixture of other groups like Turkish, Somali, Vietnamese . . . although that's the case, touch wood, there isn't a great deal of violence among or between the White and the Bangladeshi community.

A decade earlier, the pressure points were between the Bangladeshi, White and Afro-Caribbean communities. Today, the tensions are more likely to be gang related and within communities.

Where the violence tends to be now, quite often, is between different groups of Bangladeshi males and gang behaviour among young Bangladeshi males is probably one of the most difficult problems facing [the Borough] at the moment. It's one that's impacting on schools to quite a significant extent.

The causes and the factions may change but tension is constant.

When Charles Booth wrote his study of the poor in the industrial heartlands of London's East End over a century ago, he saw schools as an important part of the social transformation of the City. Education offered dreams and possibilities, scholarship and a vision of 'light breaking though the darkness', as well as practical skills which could help young people counter the grim realities of day-to-day life (Fried and Elman 1968, p. 332). The Red Bank illustration captures some of the challenges of leadership in the East End. It provides a sense of the ways in which the life of the school can be very different from the life in the streets.

To explore these issues in more depth, I have focused on three schools in the East End, a secondary school in Tower Hamlets (*Annie Besant Girls' School*), one in Hackney (*Hackney Mere*) and one in Waltham Forest (*Abbey School*). As the stories surrounding these schools unfold, they illustrate the contradictory world of London's East End. This can be a world of divisions between communities as well as a world of opportunities. There is little doubt that school matters to the children and young people. However, in crossing the threshold between street life and school life, some struggle to leave behind what holds them back. The schools themselves have adopted a range of approaches to enable young people to cross that threshold.

Leading in the East End

The physical reality

Starting at the northern tip of the East End, as I did with my journey, is Abbey School, a 11–16 high school of some 800 students, located in a dense and socially *deprived* inner-city part of area Waltham Forest. Four in five of its students are from minority ethnic groups. Waltham Forest has the fifth largest Muslim population in England and the third largest in London.

The neighbourhood around the school is one of contradictions. The area is very much part of London's history. As the area was beyond the city's walls, it was the site of plague pits and more latterly, homes to wealthy mercantile families. Walk around the back of the school's newly refurbished buildings and turn a corner. You will find a picturesque spot: a Church, a heritage site, a sixteenth-century building, an open space which beckons picnickers. However, the powerful floodlights tell another story, and while the Church may be a pleasant visitors' spot during the day, at night this is where drug dealers hang out and muggings take place.

The school draws its students from three neighbouring council estates and a large 20 story council block on the opposite side of the school to the heritage site. The sign on the estate's wall reads, 'The exercising of dogs and all ball games are prohibited': a notice of exasperation. The area has suffered from some high profile murders and gang related problems. Questions have been raised about the political messages being given by the nearby Mosque. Martin, Abbey's headteacher, was acutely aware of the day-to-day realities in the neighbourhood.

> The spaces for children to play outside safely are limited. Overcrowding, density and violence add to the stress in people's lives. Drugs and crime are problems that are getting worse.

Moving south is Hackney Mere Community School. Hackney also has its share of gang and drug-related problems. The borough is a jigsaw that is constantly being reconfigured: movements of population, regeneration, pockets of poverty. This part of Hackney also has its own patchwork of history. Sutton House, a Tudor manor dating back to the sixteenth century is nearby. Marie Lloyd and Charlie Chaplin performed at the iconic Hackney Empire. Hackney Mere has 400-plus students, aged 3–11 and is in one of the poorest areas in Europe. Thirty-five languages are spoken by its pupils who come from all over the world: Turkey, Africa, Asia, South America and Eastern Europe. 65 per cent receive free school meals. The school serves a large social housing estate characterized by an untidy meshing of styles and buildings. There is 24 h CCTV and grills on the windows of the ground floor flats. There are many single parents. Unemployment is high. There is much overcrowding and poverty, poor health and child neglect are common. Housing mobility is high for poor, refugee and immigrant families. For some, this is another transit area: a holding place through which they must pass on their way to finding another life. Some will remain, joining the established communities who watch those who pass through.

The school is located in the heart of the estate and its daily life is highly visible to the residents. The school's rooms open out onto the area's only open space. But behind the school's secure fencing is a world of possibilities. There is a buzz of energy. Yes, despite the weight of poverty, danger and hardship, Hackney Mere (in the words of its principal, Anna) 'does not feel it's a tough school, even though in the locality 'there are threads of a gang culture. There is a strong postcode sense of territory. Young people feel very vulnerable'.

Annie Besant School, Tower Hamlets, is in the heart of the old East End. The area is densely populated and the main roads are heavy with traffic. On their way to school, students walk through the busy Asian market. The school is almost hidden among the tangled streets, and its buildings provide an oasis of calm, with quiet spaces for the students to congregate, or to share lunch. These safe and secluded spaces are in stark contrast to the busy streets outside.

The school has 1,400 students, aged 11–18. More than 90 per cent are Bengali and more than 60 per cent are on free school meals. The deprivation and overcrowding that characterizes Tower Hamlets is reflected in the daily lives and experiences of many of the young women attending the school. Staff had been shocked at the overcrowding and the depth of poverty when they visited students in their homes, according to the principal, Elizabeth. Nevertheless, the young people themselves were adamant that they were not deprived. In an area with a reputation for drug-related police raids (crack-cocaine and heroin) and gangs, safety is an immediate priority for families. As Elizabeth commented:

> As a girls' school which serves a predominantly Bengali community, parents want to know 'Is my daughter going to get home safely?'

Despite the tough socio-economic conditions facing the people and neighbourhoods in which these three schools are located each school is successful.[2] Nevertheless, the gap between street life and school life is often wide, and the physical, social and political realities serve to create a testing leadership climate.

The social and political reality

The social impact of drugs and anti-social behaviour is extensive. Young people's sense of where it is safe to walk is shaped by their awareness of where drug dealers hang out and where gangs operate. Two estates which serve Abbey School have been subject to Dispersal Orders: legal orders enforced by the police, designed to stop young people from loitering or engaging in anti-social behaviour. These orders had been put in place because of drugs and intimidation but, as Martin explained, blanket bans apply to all young people on an estate, not just to those who have behaved badly but those that haven't. This breeds resentment.

Conflicting attitudes and beliefs in the different communities create a complex social and political reality for these school leaders. Martin of Abbey School, explained how the attitudes of some white working-class families made it hard for the school to establish a culture of learning:

> There's every kind of background in this school. There are mental health issues. We have a very low number of parents with any experience of Further Education or Higher Education.

Some of them are just anti-education. As the girls grow older their attendance goes down, mainly because of childcare duties. The ethnic minorities are doing very well, their parents have high ambitions for them. The problems arise with the white working-class kids.

Family breakdown is on the increase. There are often massive disputes among some of the multi-relationship families, and the children bring these disputes into school with them. We are supposed to be helping these children to achieve but we spend half our lives sorting out their social problems. Parents support their children in behaving badly. They come and tell me, 'You can't punish my child' and I have to say 'Yes I can'. Many kids in my school have a dismissive attitude towards learning, so it is difficult to maintain a culture of learning.

The relative homogeneity of the student body at Annie Besant School created its own set of challenges. There was the danger of a school with predominantly Bengali students, located in a community that was substantially Bengali, becoming culturally isolated, as Elizabeth commented:

Community, demography, politics all have an impact on what you do and how you lead and on the ethos of the school. . . (but) I sometimes feel that we are in our own bubble, and out there in London and elsewhere is a very different world.

The space which the young people inhabited within the school and within the immediate local community was monocultural. Yet, the complex world in which they had to find their way was decidedly multicultural.

The emotional reality

The impact of life on the streets was a distinctive part of the emotional reality for these school leaders. They needed to know about the kinds of pressures and stresses in the community, such as teenage pregnancies, abusive relationships, violence. However, knowing what was happening in a community but not being in a position to do anything about it was difficult, as Martin commented.

The carrying of guns is more prevalent these days. There have been some high profile murders and stabbings, high drug use and drug dealing, regular muggings. We know that there are crime hot spots. We know there are alleyways, corridors and stairwells where assaults happen.

Added to these pressures, school leaders could find themselves caught between the views and attitudes expressed in wider society and beliefs and attitudes of their students. This reinforced the importance, for Elizabeth, of creating space for students within the school to talk about controversial issues surrounding gender, race and religious identity. She talked of her own anger about how young Muslim women were all too frequently portrayed in the media.

> When Jack Straw (a national politician) made a statement about Muslim women and the hijab, a national journalist rang me up. She wanted to do a piece on the school about the hijab. I asked her 'Are you interested in our young women? Are you interested in their achievements'? It made me so angry. She wasn't interested in them at all.

The spiritual and ethical reality

Despite the pressures of the job, the rewards were incalculable. This was about 'seeing kids being successful. . . You know it's not a penance working in a school like this'. Like their colleagues in New York and South Africa, these leaders were inspired to make a difference to the lives of the young people in their charge. They wanted to make a 'positive impact on young people's lives', 'make a real difference', 'help them learn and take control of their lives'.

There was awareness of the potential for schools to challenge deep rooted beliefs and expectations, Leadership of place in the East End was about recognizing the power of conflicting forces and acknowledging the collisions between opposing ideologies but taking a stand that is based on clear moral purpose. One Principal described it in these terms:

> Before I came to this school, I remember talking to a young man about Islam. He saw it all in simple terms, Capitalism, v Islamism. There was fomentation in his madrassah leading up to

11th September 2001 about large US companies and links with Israel. It made me realise how important it was to expose young people to ideas if you wanted to prevent things happening again. There is a complexity of beliefs that young people need to be made aware of and taught how to handle.

Being and becoming a leader of this place

Given the context in which they lead, it is perhaps unsurprising that the principals were motivated by a desire to, challenge prejudice and change preconceptions. Island School, also in Tower Hamlets, had set up a project for students who had been involved in racial, faith or ethnically motivated conflict (Riley 2012). This project included a week-long residential experience in Belfast – another divided community, as the school's Principal John noted, although one divided by religion, rather than ethnicity. In Belfast the London students met with young people from the Falls Road (a Catholic area) and the Shankhill Road (a Protestant area). The project was motivated by a deep-rooted moral purpose: promoting social justice. The aim of taking the young people to Belfast was to hold up a mirror for them that reflected their own past actions in a way that challenged their preconceptions and changed behaviour.

For Anna, headteacher at Hackney Mere, moral purpose was about working to promote cohesion, both within and outside the school community. The school had been commended in a national inspection report for its work on community. Hackney Mere had sought to capitalize on the many different cultures within the school. It offered English courses for newly arrived families to help them develop their skills and make the transition into their new London-based community. It had promoted green technologies and 'Fair Trade' in ways that encouraged sustainable development, for example, through recycling and heat conservation.

The school offered a space for individual groups to meet together in a supportive environment to tackle common problems. When the groups felt stronger in their cultural identity, they would be in a position to look outwards and make connections with other groups in their neighbourhood. The school's role was to try and 'join up the dots' and make broader connections. This was about growing the roots; setting solid foundations in place in a locality which was more used to the temporary rather than the permanent. 'The soil may be thin', Anna commented, 'we try and enrich it'.

Recognizing the complex and contradictory forces in the locality, Martin had adopted two different approaches to the community challenges. The first was a strong process of engagement with the community. When I interviewed him the school was in temporary accommodation, awaiting the completion of major building works. Recognizing the ways in which a school could impinge on the local environment, as well as the ways in which that environment could impinge on a school, he had taken a personal and active role in knocking on doors and introducing herself to residents in the immediate vicinity. He had also set out to embrace all that was positive in the community:

> I see a lot about the community that is positive . . . There are festivals, concerts that are free and easily accessible. There is the Church and the library, there are Mosques that are doing things, and extended schools.

The school had a key role to play in supporting links and connections and developing local ventures with pupils, parents or the local press. His role was to encourage staff to think about the community. He held a weekly 'Surgery' to make connections with 'hard to reach groups'. He described this as creating a 'ripple effect' that could spread far beyond the centre.

The second approach was to work to protect young people from harm in the community and from influences that held them back. He worked with others to combat forced marriages and prevent young girls from missing school. In his view, for some young people, the school had to be a countervailing force.

> We used to be able to be able to maintain a barrier between life outside school and life in school. We tried to create an alternative universe for our young people, but we cannot maintain that now. They come to school in the morning with tales of such appalling experience at home, that they are simply not able to learn.

For Martin, the school gates could either act as a barrier to keep the community out, or as a gateway. The gateway was a threshold which enabled adults and young people to leave behind much that was negative in their lives and to embrace new possibilities.

For Elizabeth at Annie Besant School, the articulation of leadership of place had led to a view that it was important to give students the skills and the space to speak out. In a context in which the young Muslim women could feel that their views were alien to wider society, the school had a distinctive and challenging role: to provide them with the opportunity to voice their thoughts and beliefs. This was about helping them avoid feeling disaffected or disenfranchised, states of mind that could lead to resentment. The school offered a 'constructive environment' which provided students with the opportunity to talk about cultural issues, to express their concerns about racism and organizations such as the British National Party who were opposed to immigration. It was a 'safe place where people knew you, and staff were trained to help you', and you could work through sensitive and controversial issues that troubled you.

The school had set up a Political Forum which provided a space to talk about controversial issues. A TV channel had produced a programme about Bengali women, focusing on what they wore: the hijab (the head covering traditionally worn by many Muslim women) and the burqa (a garment that covers women completely, showing either the eyes or nothing at all). The filming had taken place on the street without the women's permission. Senior students felt that the film was an attack on them and on the Bengali community. Elizabeth explained her actions thus:

> We called a meeting to ask the girls what they thought and how they felt. If we had left it, it would have festered and become a point of dissent. . . . Our role is to give them ways to talk and the space to talk and to see how others feel about it too.
>
> Young people have a right to express themselves about how they feel. If you feel as a person that society is against you, your race, language, or your culture, it creates resentment. You have to deal with feelings, deal with them and work with them to make changes that are positive to society.

The school sets out to support local families and strengthen connections with the local community. It supports an annual community day which brings together over 3000 local people and youngsters from neighbouring primary schools. It provides a wide span of learning opportunities which brings more than 350 additional learners into the school. The school's reach went beyond the neighbourhood. It had become a lead school in London for the United Nations Association. This gave students the opportunity to travel internationally and to make key presentations to the United Nations in New York.

There were many challenges: language barriers; differences in assumptions and beliefs. Parents could be suspicious of school, worried about their daughters' lives in what, to them, was an alien environment. They often lacked experience of schools and understanding of the education system and were not confident about how to deal with school. Staff too could be hesitant to engage with communities that were very different from their own.

My place: How young people see it

Over a period of five years I have worked with just under 100 young people aged 7–17 in 12 schools in the East End, both for this book and for the project Leadership on the Front-line. I have always asked the same two questions: *What's it like living round here? What's it like being in this school?* (Riley 2008b). Some of the ways young people respond are specific to particular neighbourhoods. Other experiences seem to be common for young people across different parts of the East End. One common feature is the ways by which so many children and young people respond to the school as a physical entity, a significant building.

At Hackney Mere, the majority of children drew the school's playground and play space with loving attention. Joy (aged 7) told me 'I love playing out. There's lots we can do in the playground'. The children at Hackney Mere feel safe behind the school's mesh fence. There are many different types of equipment for them to play on. The bad thing for Joy is when it rains and she cannot play. From a child's perspective, Hackney can be a place of opportunity as well as danger. Illayda's illustration captures the two extremes of Hackney as a place of nature, full of trees and flowers, as well as a place of danger where gangs kill others and run away (Illustration 5.2).

In densely populated neighbourhoods where children live in flats, play spaces are at a premium and 'playing out' can be

ILLUSTRATION 5.2

dangerous. The playground and 'playing with my friends' becomes very important to young children like Joy. The school building itself matters. In Chapter 2 (Illustration 2.1), Amber from Tower Hamlet drew her school with loving attention. The building is beautiful and the picture is crowned by a glorious rainbow.

As children in impoverished areas grow up, they begin to recognize and experience some of the tougher aspects of city life. Some children encounter these hazards at a very young age. In Illustration 1.1 in the introduction to the book a seven-year-old child from Newham in the East End wrote, 'Newham is a dangerous borough'. The word dangerous is underscored three times.

In Chapter 1, I suggested that parts of our cities and countries' poorest areas could be 'scary' places for children and young people: places of divisions, spaces which were 'no go areas'. Undoubtedly this is the case for many children and young people in London's East End. When I met with students from Abbey School they spoke of stabbings in the area, the prevalence of gangs and intimidation by people in the hallways where they lived. I was told about someone who had been burnt with petrol and killed.

However, this is only one part of the story. There is another story too. For many young people, life is experienced as a double reality. The wider area could be intimidating, but in the immediate neighbourhood, there were people who knew you and who were friendly and helpful. There could be safety in the neighbourhood where you were known, and where you knew the parks and the shops. As Nafica illustrates, there are concerts and fun-fairs. School is a place 'where you come and learn'. However, threats can come from the known and the unknown, for there are the public places where 'it can be dangerous on your own' (Illustrations 5.3).

By and large, across all of those 100 illustrations, the school was a safe place to be which offered opportunities. There might be bullying but the threats within the school's walls were markedly different to those outside. We also gave the young people from Abbey School cameras to record what they liked in their neighbourhoods and what they disliked. We asked them to explain their choices. Their positive images included some of the open spaces in Waltham Forest. Their photographs of what worried them included the churchyard and the open space near the school described earlier and 'tagging' by local gangs.

The contrasts between life within the school's walls and life outside are vivid in the illustrations drawn by the young women

ILLUSTRATION 5.3

from Annie Besant School. Outside the school there is crime. There are guns, litter, cars, 'incidents and sad deaths', overcrowding (Illustration 5.4).

However, there is also the local market, the Mosque and multi-cultural, diverse London, with its wealth of experiences on offer, such as the London Eye on the South Bank of the River Thames. Inside the school's embrace, there are trips, the model United Nations (see Illustrations 5.5), 'the Duke of Edinburgh Award – Tiring but rewarding!!!'

While the young women from Annie Besant were uniformly positive about their school, they would have welcomed more diversity. 'We're all of the same ethnic background. We need more cultures'. The school was a place that offered them opportunities. Illustrating her experience of the school, one young woman drew a picture of herself with a smiling face at the top of a mountain and wrote:

> That's me. There's many opportunities achieved, and a mountain of work (*smiley face*)!!!!. The opportunities – debating New York, Slovenia (*amazing*). I'm here at the top of the mountain with my rucksack of work and responsibility. Lots of work and examinations (*sad face*).

ILLUSTRATION 5.4

ILLUSTRATION 5.5

As I reflect on these schools in the East End, I am struck by what an amazing and diverse city London is and how resilient its young people are. The story of young people's lives in the East End is a complex one. Some struggle to find their way in the world. Others are finding their way successfully. This was demonstrated to me in a lively academic research study of young Muslim women in the East End.

The study looked at the experiences of a group of young, predominantly Bangladeshi, women, exploring the extent to which they were becoming active change agents in their own future. This group of young women are achieving academic success. They are seeking to find a place for themselves in a complex and often alien world. The researcher asked: What are your dreams? What are your ambitions? In the following extract one young woman, Humayra, talks about a recent visit to Cambridge. She had gone there to be interviewed for a University place.

It is the day of the interview and she describes her encounter with a student 'helper'. His role for the day is to show her around. He asks her that give away question . . . 'Where are you from?' Her response is:

> I said that I was from East London . . . and he made a remark, where he just went 'oh right, oh dear' . . . And I was like, aaah that's so unwarranted, why would you say that? . . . and I thought, right, well, you can carry my bag all the way, because my bag was heavy, you know, it was full of Shakespeare, so I thought he can carry it, that's fine!
>
> (Vincent 2011)[3]

Humayra is far from being crushed by the dismissive response to her answer to the question *Where are you from?* She seeks her place in an alien world with self-assurance. She takes pleasure in the fact that the young 'helper' will have to carry her bag full of heavy Shakespeare texts for some time. Humayra won her 'place' at Cambridge. She was a student from Annie Besant. The school had played its role in developing the confidence that had enabled her to do that and to bridge very different worlds.

Some leadership learning points – Chapter 5

Given below are the five Leadership Learning Points from the chapter:

- Schools can provide newly arrived immigrants and refugees with a safe supportive space to meet together to tackle common problems. This helps them make the transition into their new community.

- The school gates can either act as a barrier to keep the community out, or as a gateway, a threshold which enables young people to leave behind what is negative in their lives.

- The impact of life on the streets is a distinctive part of the emotional reality of leadership. One aspect of leadership of place is knowing about the kinds of pressures and stresses in the community, where and how to intervene and when not to intervene.

- Schools are one of the few institutions which are in a position to recognize collisions between opposing ideologies, to challenge deep rooted beliefs and exercise leadership based on clear moral purpose.

- Students can be supported in developing their leadership in many ways, including by providing a space for them within the school to talk about difficult and controversial issues.

1 Do you agree that schools are one of the few institutions which are in a position to recognize collisions between opposing ideologies?

2 If so, what are the implications of this – For you? Your school?

3 How can the leadership of young people in your school be developed?

Notes

1 Families are eligible for free school meals if they have an income, including benefits, below £16,000 per year (BBC 2009).

2 This statement is made drawing on a range of national criteria such as test results and national inspections.

3 A doctoral student at the Institute of Education, London.

CHAPTER SIX

What's my location? – Stories from the Eastern Cape, South Africa

I may be poor like my President Mr Mandela. But I will work hard and maybe one day I will be the first black woman President of South Africa.

MOSA,
Year 10 student at Healdtown High School, Fort Beaufort,
attended by Nelson Mandela as a boy

The drive down the track to Healdtown High School from Fort Beaufort is hot and dusty. I pass a succession of one-storey houses, their yards devoid of greenery. Water is in short supply. When I enter the faded elegance of the school's buildings, my reward is Mosa. Her simple but heart-felt statement touches a chord. It speaks of hope and possibility. It points to the transformational potential of education. It reinforces the importance of schools. And it makes me think even more about the many ways that school leaders can help young people like Mosa find their way in the world.

The narrative presented in this chapter is based on schools in Nkonkobe Municipality and Fort Beaufort School District, in the heart of the Eastern Cape Province. This is one of the most impoverished rural areas in South Africa. Four out of five adults are unemployed. Employment is seasonal and concentrated into the three months of the citrus harvest. The lure of the city, for jobs and opportunities, takes many away from the locations (the rural equivalent of townships), to Port Elizabeth, Cape Town and Johannesburg.

The stories told in this chapter come from the vantage point of school leaders and students. It would be easy to tell their tales solely as ones of poverty and struggle. And of course I have reported on these. However, South Africa also has another story to tell about hope and possibilities. During my discussions with young people, I was struck by their appreciation of the support and encouragement they had received from their schools. Despite crime and poverty, HIV/Aids, there are many examples of how communities are reaching out to support their young people and to put into practice the African proverb: 'It takes a village to raise a child'. And finally, there is South Africa's history: from struggle came hope – in the future of South Africa's young people.

The story of this part of the Eastern Cape is a complex one. There is its powerful history (see BOX) and there are the current realities. The first of the seven schools I visited was Themba High School.[1] I was taken back to Belfast and a school I visited some years earlier. It served a poor community in a city divided along sectarian lines. I was struck by the disparities of wealth and poverty in the area around the school. The houses were all of the same basic design; some were dilapidated and marked by poverty, others were well-cared for; a few signalled affluence. They had gleaming paint work, big extensions and carports with expensive cars parked beneath latticed roofs. I asked the school's principal why the affluent hadn't moved out. They were the local drug dealers, he told me. Young people passed those houses every day, receiving a daily reminder that for some, crime appeared to pay.

The housing plots around Themba High School were similar in size and design to one another. Many were in a poor state of disrepair. Some showed careful attention. A small number stood out, marked by renovations and refurbishments. I asked the school's principal the same question I had asked in Belfast: why the affluent hadn't moved out. The answer was the same: the proceeds of illicit drugs and other crimes. The young people themselves understand that story. For Penisi, a Year 10 student at Themba, the 'smart' house is the one where the gangsters live (Illustration 6.1).

> Living round here is cool but there is a lot of crime which is bad . . .
>> (Me smiling) I smile because I have a good health . . .
>> (Smart house) This is the house of gangsters. . . .

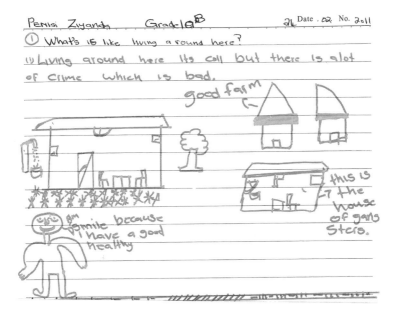

ILLUSTRATION 6.1

The story of the Eastern Cape

The Eastern Cape has a powerful story to tell. Its territories embrace the two former 'Homelands' of the Ciskei and Transkei, which became the prototype for the Bantustan system of racial segregation in the 1960s. In 1976, they were given notional 'independence' as Homelands for Xhosa-speaking South Africans. Under the Apartheid era, the Eastern Cape was divided into black, coloured and white areas, with a degree of rigidity not found in other parts of the country. Unsurprisingly, its history is one of political struggle, at the forefront of which were the anti-Apartheid leaders Nelson Mandela, Oliver Tambo, Walter Sisulu, Robert Sobwuke and Steve Biko.

The contrasts between rich and poor which characterize the region today find their origins in the colonial past. In the nineteenth century, the British drew their frontier along the Great Fish River (a 1,000 km East of Cape Town) and this became the site of what was known as the Frontier Wars, waged to keep the Xhosa people to the east of the river. Testimonies to this colonial past are the place names which are dotted about the region: Grahamstown, Fort Beaufort, Fort Hare, King William's Town, etc. The Anglo-Boer Wars of 1899–1902, fought between Britain and descendants of the Dutch settlers living in the two Boer Republics of the South African Republic (Transvaal) and the Orange Free State, also form part of the Eastern Cape's history.

In the pre-Apartheid era, education in the Eastern Cape was organized by six education departments, each responsible for different racial categories: an administrative arrangement generated by the Bantustan system of racial segregation which created separate territories for different racial groups, uprooting and dividing many families. While the Apartheid resettlement process severed connections from land and place for many communities, it also created the opportunity for some racial groups to reassert their identity. Dominick, the school principal of Tumelo Church School, described his family's experience in the following terms:

> My grandparents lived in the centre of town (Fort Beaufort). Then they were removed and dumped here . . . But it taught us a lesson . . . to be independent and strong and to be proud. But we could not enjoy what whites enjoyed. After matriculation, I wanted to become a furniture maker . . . But I was turned away . . . I couldn't become a furniture maker because it was a reserved job – but I could be carpenter. Later I trained as a woodwork teacher. And as I grew up, (this location) became a proud place to be.

Between 1994 and 1997, the functions and responsibilities of the six education departments were transferred to a new education department. Today, there are regional problems around funding, consistency of leadership, union interference and alleged corruption, which create significant challenges for schools in the Eastern Cape. Access to schools is determined by proximity, language (English, Afrikaans or Xhosa) and money. All but a few schools in the most economically deprived areas charge fees, and fee levels in the formerly white schools are beyond the means of most of those living in the locations – the rural equivalent of townships. As a consequence, and with a few exceptions, schools remain largely segregated along racial lines.

The realities of leadership

I've got a dream but the resources to deliver that dream are so limited.

(Lerato, school leader)

Leadership in challenging contexts is an intensely complex and personal activity, and no more so than in the Eastern Cape. The reality of the social and economic context which characterizes Nkonkobe puts school leaders to the test. The physical realities are extreme. The social and political problems are seemingly unsolvable. The challenges test the emotional resilience of the leaders, their personal beliefs and commitments to the learners in their charge.

The physical reality

The realities of leadership in this part of the Eastern Cape include the practical daily challenges of battling for basic resources and equipment as well as managing student numbers. Class size can vary from 20 to 50, and many schools are facing a reduced student population and significant changes in staffing levels. Managing the infrastructure is an ongoing struggle, and the quality of the school buildings varies significantly. One of the schools I visited lacked electricity, several had no running water. Leaking roofs are endemic. Computers are highly valued, but in short supply, and internet access can be limited and expensive. Where internet access does exist, it is likely to be paid for by a charity and its usage limited to senior staff. Mpho, a school leader at Uuko Secondary School, described the challenges being faced in the IT department thus:

> We've a shortage of resources, e.g. computers, and limited science equipment. We had a number of computers donated but only four are working now. We ran a computing course on how to solve computer problems but we've had to abandon that. Our plan had been to teach learners marketable skills. But teachers themselves are not computer literate. The library is small which makes it hard to encourage reading. We'd like to have library resources to house historical documents about President Mandela.

The physical realities also include the illnesses and threats that children encounter every day. Drugs and violence plague their neighbourhoods. HIV/AIDS has a major effect on health, well-being, family lives, futures and expectations. In some locations, as many as one in five may be infected. HIV/AIDS also has a significant impact on schools and on educational opportunities. Here is Bambiso's description of the realities of his life in South Africa. Bambiso is a pupil at Kagisu Primary School.

> In our country there is HIV and drugs and prostitution. There are many people without food and water. Without Education there is no job. Without Education, there is nothing.

Schools have to accommodate the needs of children who have to rest after taking anti-viral drugs, or who are overburdened with the domestic pressures of looking after siblings. Staff become infected, with all of the practical and emotional consequences that this entails. Tau, principal of Themba High School described the challenges of HIV/AIDS in the following terms:

> We had a black couple who adopted some AIDS children and the kids are here . . . It was a big thing when we enrolled them . . . 10 kids. Everyone knew. Staff and children were all scared to start

with . . . but after we had a workshop with staff, and we attended courses, we all became easier dealing with the issues. The children are all on treatment, they take it at home.

But we've had other issues too; parents dying. Last year, we had two cases and we had to go to social offices because we couldn't leave them [the young people) on their own. They went into foster car . . . You get other cases where our learners may have an older brother or sister in the city but during the week they are alone. It affects their school work and behaviour.

Throughout the locations, there are high numbers of single-parent families, families divided because parents are working away, and many young people live with grandparents. Poverty and poor health are widespread. Children may arrive at school with empty stomachs, having walked 7 or 8 km to get there.[2] Unsurprisingly, they lose their concentration, as Mpho, a school leader from Uuko Secondary School, commented:

Parents don't have jobs and struggle for food. It's a very disadvantaged area and families de-motivated. They don't help learners because of their own illiteracy and there is no model for learners about what they can do if they get their matriculation.

She went on to explain about the ways in which the restrictions of students' home lives limited their educational experiences.

The quality of learning is limited. Learners find it hard to theorise. They've had no experience of that and it interferes with their learning. There are limited opportunities to progress to University. Our learners don't have access, or understanding of what could be done and how.

The social and political reality

The social and political reality of leadership in the Eastern Cape is shaped by the political realities as well as by the socio-economic conditions that constrain young people's lives. Political realities include national policies as well as the policies and practices of a struggling District Administration. Relationships between schools and officers from the local administration are uneasy, with school leaders expressing their sense of isolation and staff feeling resentful of limited opportunities for promotion (with some suggestions that promotion is linked to the local political machinery and union membership), of restricted developmental opportunities and of plans to reduce staffing levels.

The politics of Apartheid continue to shape the social and political reality. For example, the location around Kagiso Primary was settled in 1997, in the immediate post-Apartheid era, and provided an opportunity for families to take some land and develop it for themselves. Today, unemployment is endemic and the availability of drugs and alcohol (particularly cheap wine) an attraction for many. A shebeen (illegal bar) sprang up on the school's doorstep and was finally removed after police intervention (Illustration 6.2).

Housing is a mixed bag, with some good quality housing belonging to teachers and other professional staff, in close proximity to poor single room dwellings. Local transport is erratic and 1 in 4 young people walk to school (5 km each way). Lack of transport reduces opportunities in a number of ways, such as making it difficult for schools to play each other at sport.

The challenges for Kagiso Primary, as for many other schools, spring up from a community living with severe poverty and facing limited opportunities. There is high mobility: parents move around

ILLUSTRATION 6.2

for work, so children find themselves moving from school to school. The 'place' itself is one of the challenges, as the lack of privacy and density of population encourages early sexualization. According to Siphiwe, one of the school's leaders:

> It is not a comfortable place for them (young learners). Children see more than they should as young learners. When they are living in one room shacks, they see everything . . . Our learners tell us what happens out there . . . We called a meeting of the parents to talk about this and there have been big changes. Some families have built another room; others have moved their children to other families nearby who have more space for them.

High poverty levels and the prevalence of HIV (AIDS) means that the school needs to attend to the basic nutrition, health and diet of its young learners. The school has a small garden, drawn with great care and loving attention by a number of children, and the food grown is used to supplement the basic meal provided in the school (Illustration 6.3). However, the funding for basic nutrition may not be available in the future: a casualty of the financial pressures facing national government. Some of the most vulnerable of young learners may miss out even more in the future.

For the young learners at Kagiso Primary, alcohol, drugs, crime and theft are unwelcome features of everyday life; lack of water a regular hardship. But there is also much to value, as Thomas explained:

> The good thing about this place is being loyal and the most important thing is love. It's a good family, good friends, education, sport . . . And there are bad things that don't make me feel good . . . drugs, alcohol, HIV, small schools, unemployment.

Some, such as Zozi, were more critical about the limitations of everyday school life:

> In our school we don't have enough classes, and we want to learn a lot, and don't have netball and soccer kits, and we want to learn a lot of things in our schools, so we want you to give us the netball kit, and we do not want alcohol in our schools and drugs.

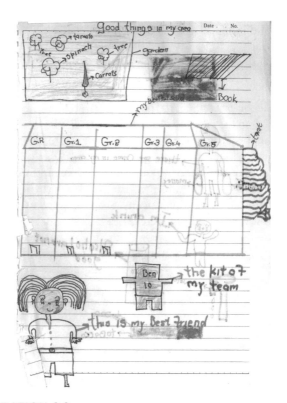

ILLUSTRATION 6.3

In the social and economic circumstances which characterize the locations of this part of the Eastern Cape, many children are vulnerable. Children with special needs such as learning difficulties are particularly vulnerable to physical and sexual abuse, and to unwanted early pregnancies. According to Baruti, Head of a Day Care Centre, when families find that their children have special needs, they tend to blame each other.

> We sit down with parents and try and tell them what we can do, and what their children can do. . . . These kids are a misfortune for their parents. Some of them abuse their children and do little to help their social development. Doctors make sure that the child is getting their disability allowance but parents misuse that and the children don't come to school. They're not interested

in the child. Siblings get the money, or the clothing allowances. These young people are used to fetch and carry, this includes delivering drugs.

The emotional reality

The emotional reality of leadership in the Eastern Cape is tied to some of these political realities. School leaders have aspirations but struggle to deliver them, and are caught between supporting national policy objectives (which they may sign up to in principle) and the implementation of those policies, given the realities on the ground. The administrative holdups which appear to characterize the district office can get in the way of the achievement of basic objectives, such as feeding children. As one school leader complained: 'there was no one there (district office) to sign off the cheque for the nutritional programme'.

Proposals to reduce staffing levels have created a sense of defeat among some teachers that is palpable and school principals are caught in the firing line. They have to manage those emotions as well as the expectations of local administrators. Tau, school principal of Themba High School, put this sanguinely:

> By and large the teachers are well trained but the many changes in the curriculum make it difficult. The problem is that we have all these changes but there is not enough funding. For example, the government introduced life orientation skills and the NCS (National Curriculum Statement) and this means the teachers are faced with the challenges of having to teach higher standards and grades.
>
> The ANC did a lot of research on education in different parts of the world, introduced initiatives that countries claimed to have been successful and then have tried to apply them to this country, but without the necessary resources. For example, outcome-based education has been dropped because of the challenges. The resources were not there, particularly in rural areas. The initiative became a burden for teachers. Changing the syllabus time and time again has killed teachers' morale. I give them a list of workshops and they say 'not again!'

The spiritual and ethical reality

The spiritual and ethical reality is that sense of what drives or motivates school leaders. It is the hardest reality to catch sight of and hold on to. The school leaders and principals I met each have their own story to tell of hard work, perseverance, endeavour and giving back to communities. Having benefited from education and the opportunities that can flow from it, enabling others to succeed was a driving force in their leadership. Dominick, principal of Tumelo Church School expressed his personal commitment in the following terms:

> I have a love and passion for teaching: a passion to educate, a passion to lead under difficult circumstances.

Baruti, head of the Day Care Centre, was inspired to take on a difficult and challenging role by a commitment to unleash the talents of young people with special needs and to encourage them to be self-reliant, in a context in which many were rejected by their own families.

Capturing what motivates school leaders – particularly what those ethical and social drivers are – is difficult. The following two case studies (one primary school and one secondary) encapsulate the challenges of leadership in the Eastern Cape. The stories, as told by school leaders and principals, are juxtaposed with the views and perceptions of the young people in their schools. The case studies exemplify the realities of leadership in challenging contexts, the emotional responses of school principals and school leaders to some of those challenges, and the ways in which leadership needs to be grounded in school leaders' own sense of values and purpose.

Leadership in practice

Themba high school

Themba High School has 407 students and, as a school serving a highly impoverished community, has a small delegated budget. The challenges of creating a positive learning environment are significant. In 2005, a major storm damaged the roofs of several classrooms and wrecked the sewage system, depriving the school of its toilet facilities. According to the Principal of Themba High, Tau, this has created 'major health issues and embarrassment for young women'. From the students' perspective, the major concerns about their school are related to the physical conditions: ('what I don't like is that when it's cold the windows are broken and we get cold too and toilets'). The comment, 'I don't like my school because we don't have no toilets', was a typical one.

There are a number of recurring images in the illustrations drawn by the young people. They are positive about their school and their teachers ('if you have a problem you can talk to your teacher about it') and there are many images of sporting activities, but there are shared concerns about the behaviour of some fellow students. 'I don't like . . . the children that not like school, so there's bad children, like boys who do smoking and do not do homework. I don't like children who don't go to school'. Andiswo's assessment of school life is fairly typical:

> Good things about my school . . . You are given an opportunity to express your feelings; you even learn some things you didn't know; if you have a problem you can talk to your teacher about it; teachers are so understanding. . . .
>
> Bad things . . . There is a problem of teenage pregnancy; children are smoking at an early stage; children are dropping out of school.
>
> Life round here: Around here people are sharing what they have with other people so that they don't starve to death.

From the perspective of teachers and school leaders, there is a disparity between what the school would like to offer and what it can provide. Tau described this tension in the following terms:

> (Our young people) are living in a world in which the first time a child gets to use a computer is in school. The use in school is restricted by the number of computers and the limited internet access. They don't get to use computers at home. To be computer literate means having regular access and being able to work on things and problem solve . . . You can take a child who is really capable but because of the lack of resources that child will struggle.

This is an area in which the majority of people are semi-literate and few people are working, and as a consequence, education is not seen as being particularly important. You can't blame the parents but if a child needs help with school, there is no one to do this. Children struggle to understand basic concepts; it takes far longer here because of the lack of experiences in their lives.

Because of poverty and all of the health hazards the children get sick. They are vulnerable to TB due to exposure and poverty. If you educate sick people, they struggle to learn.

There's also HIV and Aids which has significant consequences for the community. People are involved in sexual activity to get money. Some children end up living on their own and the mortality of one or both parents means that the learners become parents to their brothers and sisters.

The location is in transition, with established families moving out to access low cost housing recently built by the Government on the outskirts of major towns, such as Alice. While the new accommodation provides improved basic facilities, families have lost the social networks and connections that village life has to offer, and this has particular impact on the many single parents in the area. Mafuane, a school leader from Themba who lived locally, described the dislocations in the community created by this churning process.

Some of the people round here are born and bred, others have come into the neighbourhood. Some are proud of this place, others don't care. This school is surrounded by the location. Many burglaries have taken place and people don't feel they own the place. There are some people who act responsibly. Some of the intruders come from the surrounding farms. Because of government policies, there is movement. People move away for the housing.

The notions of churning, instability and change are reflected in young people's accounts of their lives. For example, Tokwe describes her daily life on the location where she experiences the challenges of housing: movement, overcrowding, lack of privacy. These challenges add to her appreciation of the opportunities that school life has to offer and to her recognition of the ways in which the behaviour of the streets can spill into the behaviours of the playground.

> Shops is very important to buy something . . . because sometimes we can't afford to go to town that's why I like shops. . . .
>
> I don't like our house because we stay in small houses and we can't make our garden and we can't stay with our animal. Sometimes we stay with lots of people in one house and then no one can breathe and we get diseases easily. . . .
>
> School: I don't like people who are fighting at school because we are brothers and sisters at this school. . . . I like to learn, especially maths, here at school; we get a good education; our teachers is very kind, understanding teacher (Illustration 6.4).

The illustrations drawn by young people from Themba about their lives on the location include recurring images of fights, stealing, smoking and drinking: 'Children are drinking, children are doing

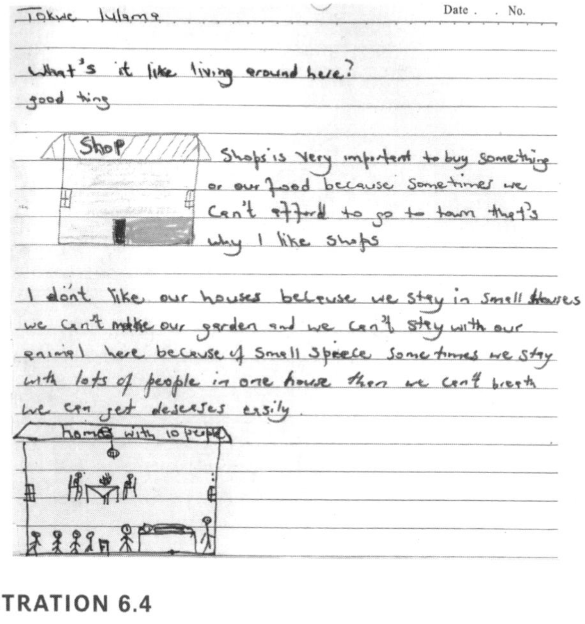

ILLUSTRATION 6.4

drugs, children are stealing in the streets and towns', one student commented. From the young people's perspective there are major infrastructure issues. Images include dripping taps and the comment: 'I don't like the waste of water because it's very important in our community'. Other comments included: 'I don't like it when the rain is coming because there are holes in the road'.

Comments and illustrations from Nolubabalo and Jezi demonstrate the complexities of life. Both young people acknowledge the negatives of life in the location, but they also point to many positives features, possibly more than those observed by their teachers.

> *Nolubabalo*: It is good to live here. We have different cultures and heritage days and festivities). . . .
>
> What I don't like about living round here is teenagers getting pregnant at a young age and drinking some time and then using drugs too.
>
> *Jezi*: Living round here is Good because we have lots of activity that we usually do and Beautiful houses and tree, shops, and many schools, and there are also bad things like people fighting . . . What I like being in this school is that we learn lots of things and we even have sports events and I enjoy being in School because I can play, sing, write, and even do drama (Illustration 6.5).

Responding to these kinds of challenges as a leader, Tau argued, means acknowledging the realities for young people while also working to develop active responses that can be meaningful to their lives. It also means recognizing the vital role of the school, not only as a place of educational opportunities but also as a place that demonstrates alternative ways of living and being.

> I'm not a social worker but the reality is that schools must have plans for children who have nothing. Their progress in schools is affected mentally and physically by what happens to them every day. There are issues of early pregnancy – not so many here, but one of the local schools has a high incidence of this.
>
> There is a culture of theft. (Young people) get involved in drugs and stealing to buy their drugs. Only yesterday, I had a visit from

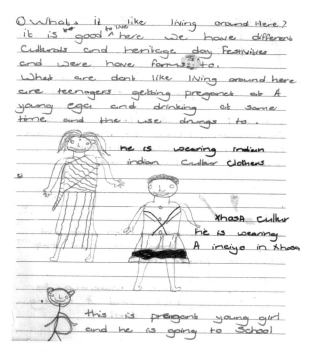

Q what is it like living around Here?
it is to we good here we have different
Cultrals and heritage day Festivities
and were have forms to.
What are dont like living around here
are teenagers getting pregonck at A
young ege and drinking at some
time and the use drungs to.

he is wearing indian
indian Cultur Clothers

Xhasa Cultur
he is wearing
A inciyo in Xhosa

this is pregonb young girl
and he is going to School

ILLUSTRATION 6.5

the police about a boy who had stolen a DVD from someone who was deceased. I helped them track him down. We have to solve these sorts of things. Stealing starts at an early age (Grade 4, Primary) and we need to tackle this. The other day, children broke in through the roof of a local school and stole things. We have to make our expectations high here and show them that stealing is not the way forward and the way out of things.

Partnerships between the school and the community were vital and could have a powerful impact. Not all of the 'smart' houses belonged to 'gangsters'. A number of teachers and other professional workers also lived locally which gave young people alternative role models to choose from: role models who could demonstrate the benefits of education and hard work. For Tau, it was critical that schools engaged actively with their local community to present an alternative reality and demonstrate that while the lure of the streets could be strong, the benefits while immediately attractive were short-lived.

> We go to the community and call on local people to come and give a talk about how to approach life. We call on people who are exemplary, who are role models in society. We try to make it clear to our learners that what they do has an effect on others. Stealing from others is only a temporary way out of poverty. But it's hard for the child who goes home hungry. Going to jail is a bad start.
>   We show (the learners) the importance of education. Give practical examples of people who have made a success, who've got a job and have made something of themselves. To motivate them we say that doing crime makes a joy which is temporary. In the long run, it doesn't work.

I arrived at Themba High School with staff from the Borien Foundation and officers from the school district. The plan had been to view the roof that had been in a state of disrepair since 2005, ahead of refurbishment. But a major part of the roof had been repaired. Working with the local community and drawing on the small resources available to the school, the principal had taken unilateral action. At a later point, we discussed what made a good school principal. I told him about work I had undertaken in the United Kingdom which had found that some of the best school principals were rule breakers. He roared with laughter.

Thandiwe primary school

Thandiwe Primary School is near Fort Beaufort in the centre of a location which has a neglected air about it. The prevailing colour is grey. Little appears to grow. There are few trees and little greenery. The same contrasts are visible in the housing as seen in the location surrounding Themba High School. Some houses are semi-derelict; others have been extended, or are in the throes of major building works. Amenities are few.

To an outsider, the location appears bleak and barren, but as Lesedi, the school principal explained, it also offers people a place to be themselves, reinforcing a sense of identity and offering possibilities. He described the political significance of the location in the following terms:

> It is a stony area with thin soil. People came and planted gardens and tried to build a foundation for themselves. (In the Apartheid era) there was a separation of people, black and coloureds in different places. . . .
> I was brought up on a farm. If you didn't greet the farmer, if you didn't open the gate for him, he would say to your father, 'Why doesn't your child know how to behave?' Coming to this location was good for me. My parents were virtual slaves on the farm. Here I got a chance to go to school and I became a teacher. Education is very important here . . . The locations offer freedom and opportunities for education.

Thandiwe Primary School is a no fees schools, designated as having exceptionally high levels of poverty and social need.[3] It is also unusual in that it also has a delegated budget to cover basic books and equipment. Poverty is endemic. School attendance can be irregular as many children have nothing to eat. Lesedi described the challenges thus:

> HIV (AIDS) is a big issue. It disorientates the lives of our learners. You have children left at home on their own because one or both parents have died. Maybe she's 11 or 12 and she has to do all the cooking and look after brothers and sisters and on top of that there is the school work. . . .
> Unemployment is very high. Work is seasonal on the farms, only three months a year – June, July and August – that's for picking citrus fruit.
> Parents get allowances, basic subsistence for their children, 250 rand, per child, per month. The problem here in South Africa is that the parents drink a lot and there is a big problem of teenagers drinking and taking drugs. There's drug abuse. The parents go to loan sharks to borrow money and they use their allowance to buy alcohol. The sharks charge huge interest and they come and take the card for the child's allowance to get their money back.

The starkness of the location was characterized by the lack of running water throughout the location and at the school.

There's been no running water at the school or on the location. The taps are not working. The garden at the school has died. The school collects rain water in tanks but one of the tanks is not working properly. When they run out of water, people have to pay the Municipality for a delivery.

I asked Lesedi the question: 'Why do you not have water?' and received this reply:

In South Africa we have problems with the Municipality. All the time they are fighting. The Councillors get paid – good salaries (46,000 rand) – and so they fight for the job and there is no one to make sure the services are good. Everyone wants to be a councillor and it works against the country. There are powerful fights at the local level and water is highly political . . . The ruling Party (ANC) suspended some local councillors. While the fighting takes place, the service delivery doesn't happen . . .

According to Lesedi, the lack of running water creates many problems for the school, including lack of toilet facilities. Political battles in the location have created a climate of intolerance and the daily crime has generated further insecurities.

A year ago, there was no street lighting in this area. There is now lighting but you need to keep inside your house after dark. People break into each others' houses. The local church has been battered three times. It can be a difficult and scary place to live.

The children in the school illustrate their lives with a series of consistent images. There are positive images related to the provision of new housing by the Government, such as these from Khatywa, who wrote:

In the Fort Beaufort we have RDP (Government) houses for free and for mahala. I like to stay in Fort Beaufort because it is nice . . . This is my mother and I love her and other people and I love all the people in my country (Illustration 6.6).

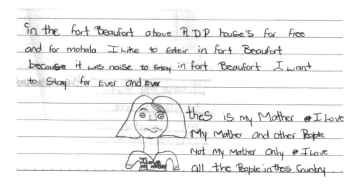

In the fort Beaufort above RDP house's for free
and for mohala I Like to steir in fort Beaufort
because it was noise to stay in fort Beaufort I want
to stay for Ever and Ever

thes is my Mother & I Love
My Mother and other People
Not my Mother Only & I Love
all the People in thes Country

ILLUSTRATION 6.6

The school itself is drawn with love and attention and the sports facilities are a source of pleasure. Good aspects of school include the classes, the teachers, the nurses, the social workers. The playground is alive with activities. Some of the children included a list of 'dos', such as clean your school and clean your body, and 'don'ts', such as don't get pregnant. Other items of importance to the young learners were:

- *When someone does not have nothing, don't let him cry.*
- *This is my school table and chair and books.*
- *I like playing cricket.*
- *I love my teachers because it helps me every day.*
- (Picture) This is me *playing and laughing . . . I like to play with other children, even if they are poor; we like sister and brother because we are of the same blood.*
- *You don't smoke in school, and teachers must give children respect.*
- *I like to wear the uniform, and do the right thing.*

Within the location, there are many images of rubbish, bad language, smoking, fighting, hijacking of vehicles, and frequent illustrations of guns, with comments such as, 'I don't like strangers because they kill me and you'. Many homes are drawn with loving attention, and comments accompanying the drawings include these from Sinalo:

> I like living in Fort Beaufort because we're not those who killed. They're families in peace, like playing with each other. 'Don't be aggressive, be a child who has respect in his family and the others cultures . . . I don't like those who break windows, stealing and abusing other children.

The school – its leaders and the whole staff – are united in their attempts to provide an alternative vision of possibilities and opportunities. Displayed on the walls of the Principal's office are the school's plans and aspirations; the Learners' Code of Conduct; 'Our Prouds' and 'Our Sorries' and the solutions to these. The school's Mission Statement is prominent:

> This public school is committed to working jointly with the community in ensuring the best education. We aim to provide the necessary resources, to work in teams, be supportive, trustworthy, to prepare our learners to enter on careers of their choice, as responsible citizens who will be creators of the new job seekers.

I met briefly with the teaching staff and asked them what they were most proud of. One member of staff said, 'I am proud to be a teacher in this school. I am here to serve my community'.

While the challenges might appear insurmountable, they are tackled with a practical air. A food scheme is established. Employing a bank of local cleaners to work in the school ensures that some money gets fed back into the community. But the school's vegetable patch had had to be abandoned because there is no water and the school has no solution to the lack of running water and absence of decent toilets.

Being and becoming a leader of this place

> To be a leader people here you need to understand others. . . .
> You need to go out and understand community issues.
>
> (Siphiwe, school leader, Kagisu Primary)

One of the striking features of the leadership story in this part of the Eastern Cape is the ways in which, and the extent to which, the principals and school leaders reach out to their communities. This can include active participation in local forums (such as a Township Education Forum) with teachers, the community, parents, business and health workers. Participation is seen as an integral part of the job in order to 'rev up this community' or to 'work towards a dream'. One school was trying to raise money to build a theatre and resource centre for the children and wider community, with all of the labour for this enterprise being provided by the local community. Dominick, the school principal from Tumelo Church School described this approach in the following terms:

> There are many new challenges post 1994. I have learned that to secure good leadership, I must forge relationship with parents and the community. You have to force them to respect you. They have to see you as a role model. This means being involved in community activities, local bodies, the church, serving on the museum board, actively being involved in the community. By doing so, teachers will join me on the wagon.

Being and becoming a leader requires a high degree of personal commitment. This is about going beyond what is expected – going that extra mile – in order to create a sense of possibilities. Siphiwe, a school leader from Kagisu Primary, saw it in the following terms:

> You have to try and tell them what is important for them for their future. You have to give them a sense of possibilities. I've take some of them to my own home to show them what is possible.

She explained what motivated her:

> What I like is progress. I like to see people making progress. Most of the time you are with people who are ordinary and the joy is persuading them to try, no matter how hard the difficulties are, to rise above them.

Siphiwe had wanted to demonstrate to the children and young people in her school that they could create opportunities for themselves, without relying on the Government. She worked with members of the community to set up a small workers' co-operative which draws on the skills of local women in beadwork. Learners and members of the community work together to make handicrafts which are then sold in the towns. The project develops the skills of the young people, builds local capacity and develops confidence and a belief in self-reliance.

Essential to these working relationships is trust. Leadership in these difficult conditions is about growing trust and learning to trust. It is about building confidence in young people about what they can achieve. In a tightly knit community, school leaders needed to know when to intervene and when to let events take their course: when to keep private what a learner had told them and when to talk to their families. This comes down to understanding young people's lives. It also means going beyond: going that extra mile. The reward is watching young people soar.

Some leadership learning points – Chapter 6

Given below are the five Leadership Learning Points from the chapter:

- Churning and instability are re-occurring features of young people's lives. Schools need to be places of absolute safety where young people's needs are paramount and where they know what to expect – and are not disappointed.

- If schools are to offer young people the opportunities they deserve, reaching out and connecting to communities and building social capital is not an optional extra.

- Leaders of place recognize the realities of young people's lives, engage with the social challenges which young people encounter on the streets and offer alternatives.

- Being and becoming a leader in an area of extreme social disadvantage requires high degrees of personal commitment, a determination to go the extra mile and a willingness to 'bend' the rules for the good of young people.

- Recognizing the leadership potential of young people and building their self-reliance is a key leadership task.

1 Is your school a safe place for young people?

2 Does it engage with the social challenges which young people encounter on the streets and offer alternatives?

3 When should leaders bend the rules?

Notes

1 The visit was facilitated by the Borien Educational Foundation for Southern Africa (BEFSA) which works to help reduce poverty in some of the poorest communities in South Africa: see www.befsa. co.uk. Interviews or structured discussions took place with four school principals, two deputy principals, or acting principals, two other school leaders (referred to as school leaders), and twelve other members of staff. One hundred and sixteen young people contributed to the drawing exercise and the linked discussions with them. Fifty-eight were from secondary schools and forty-eight from primary. The analysis also draws on discussions with a range of meetings and workshops with school leaders working with BEFSA.

2 The national government has attempted to deal with the travel issue by providing a number of yellow bicycles in the district for children who have a distance to travel. While the numbers are limited, the project has been welcomed, even though there are concerns about safety and security.

3 The majority of school in South Africa charge additional fees. For example, the formerly white school of Wintersberg in the Eastern Cape charges 800 rand/month.

CHAPTER SEVEN

A place in this world

In *West Side Story*, set in 1950s' New York, rival gangs, the Puerto Rican Sharks and the white Jets, struggle for dominance of the streets. Star-crossed lovers Tony and Maria find themselves on opposing sides of this bitter divide. The place they seek is one where they can be who they are and not who or what they are labelled.

West Side Story was a hit. Its onstage gritty realism captured the struggle of life on the street. Offstage, director Jerome Robbins kept the two rival gangs apart, maintaining the performers' onstage edge by posting newspaper clippings of real gang violence on the backstage bulletin board (Long 2003).

Battles between gangs or posses are not new – in everyday life or in fiction. Fear of gangs looms large for many of the young people whose stories have found a place in this book. In fiction, as in real life, the names of the gangs and their ethnic origin may change but the essential drama is the same. In *Romeo and Juliet*, the Montagues fight the Capulets. *West Side Story* started out as East Side Story. The original plot was based on conflict between an Irish American Roman Catholic family and a Jewish family: the setting, the Lower East Side of Manhattan, during the Easter–Passover season (ibid).

The fight for space and territory can take place on the street or in the school playground. The conflict is often between established communities and new ones. However, turf wars are no longer a male preserve. In Brooklyn's East School, the struggle for space and territory was between its growing African-American community and their more established Hispanic 'sisters'. 'We're not going to have West Side Story here', school principal Lena announced with grim determination.

Fights for turf are not the only ways that young people can experience their lives as divided. The divisions can be between street life and school life, between those who have money and those who don't. Divisions can be based on perceived or actual differences between immigrant and long-standing residents or between groups of different faiths or political allegiances. Divisions restrict young people's views and perceptions of what is possible. All too often, these divisions emerge because the parties don't understand each other or lack shared experience. What was striking about the origins of the 2001 race riots in England's Northern towns (discussed in Chapter 1) was the degree to which the two communities in conflict with each other – white and Asian – lived separate lives.

Being and becoming a leader of place

Recalibrating leadership

The stories told in this book signpost the many ways in which schools hold a significant place in the lives of young people. They provide examples of how school leaders respond to the complex and demanding lives of the young people in their care. The challenge is to recognize what some young people, such as Dyamiyi from South Africa, may have to contend with (Illustration 7.1) and open up the routes to their success (Illustration 7.2).

Throughout the rest of this chapter, I want to illustrate how leadership of place can be enacted in the spaces both within and outside the school. Young people can give us some important clues about how to do this.

In *Whose School is it Anyway?* (Riley 1998), I suggested that school leadership was intrinsically bound in context: global-, national-, local- and school-based. I included the following advert for a headteacher. It was written by a group of 9-year-olds who worked with me in a project on school leadership in England, Scotland and Denmark (MacBeath et al. 1996).

Headteacher Wanted

Come to our school. It is a good school. The teachers are good, the children will welcome you and everyone will treat you well.

If you are going to apply for this job, you will have to be able to communicate with children, be respectful of them and understand their point of view. You will need to be qualified and experienced.

ILLUSTRATION 7.1

ILLUSTRATION 7.2

You will need to be energetic and, outgoing, confident, mix with people easily and understand their feelings. You will need to be able to understand other people's beliefs and be a calming influence on the school.
Try your luck and be the best!

(Riley 1998, p. 120)

The same group of children also wrote a job description. The two together encapsulate some important ingredients of leadership of place. Their job description emphasized *respect*. It was important 'Not to be racist' and to make 'others see that the colour of their skin doesn't matter'. The headteacher had to instil *confidence* in the wider community as well as in the school. S/he 'must be able to make children, adults and the community confident about the things they do in school'.

The children wrote about *communication* and the need to 'keep in touch with the local community, letting them know what is happening in the school'. They emphasized *responsibility*: 'You need to know how to take responsibility for things happening in the school and not blame others'. They identified the importance of shaping the climate of the school and creating bridges with the local community in ways that enabled them to find a place where they could feel safe, where they could feel they belonged. The headteacher, they said, needed to 'know how to look after the building and create a nice environment and a safe place for children' (Riley 1998, p. 121).

In the years since I wrote that book, there have been significant changes in the ways in which governments across the globe have come to view the role of schools and their leaders. The introduction of high stakes accountability, tests and quasi-markets has undoubtedly created significant pressures on schools and their leaders. Yet, the stories presented in this book suggest that leaders of place frequently operate outside the more conventional codes of behaviour expected of school leaders. They challenge prejudices and preconceptions: John from Island School in Tower Hamlets took students involved in racial, faith or ethnically motivated conflict to Belfast. They take control when the system isn't working: Tau at Themba High School in South Africa got the school's roof mended 'unofficially'. They intervene when others might have stood back: Carla at Downtown in Brooklyn 'semi-adopted' a young woman who had been raped and was threatening to kill herself.

These leaders fully recognize the importance of achieving good examination grades for young people from highly disadvantaged communities. However, their leadership objectives, as well as their actions, go far beyond this goal. When I interviewed headteachers and school principals for the three locality studies, I asked them for examples of actions they had taken in recent days which they associated with leadership of place. These included:

- *Reaching out to the community*: taking part in a planning meeting at a neighbouring school for a conference on encouraging learning in the local community

- *Bringing the community into the school*: a review meeting to discuss a new scheme to bring local people into the school to act as role models to students

- *Challenging street life*: a series of meetings with students who had been in trouble to challenge their behaviour on the streets and ask the question: Do you want to be hanging around on the streets ten years from now?

- *Enabling young people to see their place in society*: meeting with school staff and the British Legion to plan a visit to the battlefields of World War I. The purpose was to help young people understand new aspects of Britain's past, such as the role of the army of Indians who serviced battle. At Flanders, Sherpas picked up the dead bodies so that the battle could recommence. Many were killed by exploding mines.

By their actions, these leaders strengthen the connections between the world outside the school and the world within. Their focus on young people's identity, lives and experiences helps those youngsters find their place in the school and in their communities. In political climates which have a strong focus on centrally directed and highly specific performance targets, leadership of place is about seeing the bigger picture. It is about recognizing the broader needs of young people and the importance of their sense of self-worth. School leaders' commitment, energy and focus to do this springs from a sense of moral purpose. It is based on the desire to see a very different world for young people.

The notion of leadership of place which is emerging in this book is linked to other concepts of leadership, as shown in Box X. What all of these notions have in common, with each other and leadership of place, are *agency* and *shared action*. There is a recognition that whatever the boundaries and expectations within a school system, school leaders at every level within a school can choose to exert their influence and work with others to meet young people's needs.

Identity and meaning

Our complex and modern world has expanded our notion of what we mean by identity. Issues related to gender, ethnicity, religion and culture are now all part of the daily diet fed to us by newspapers and television. Young people seek their own identity. They can be drawn into movements that encourage them to take responsibility as a global citizen. Equally too, they can be drawn into a world of extremist ideologies.

BOX X

- *Stewardship*: the notion of looking after the well-being of the school on behalf of others in the school and in the local community (Murphy and Louis 1994): an approach emphasized by the children who wrote the job description

- *Leadership of, and for, learning*: connecting the qualities of leadership to the nature of schools as authentic places of learning (MacBeath and Dempster 2009)

- *Tribal leadership*: building pride and developing relationships within the 'tribe', with the aim of creating a shared culture and a sense of belonging (Logan et al. 2008)

- *Advocacy leadership*: reconfiguring schools to meet the needs of particular groups of young people. In the United Kingdom, this notion has centred on the potential for Children's Centres and local agencies to work together in locally based collaborative structures organized around the needs of children and young families (Ranson and Crouch 2009). In the United States, the focus has been on social justice and shifting power to students and communities, particularly in low-income communities of colour (Anderson 2009).

Modern life is more uncertain, more fluid than life in the past. Zygmunt Bauman writes of the shift from solid times to liquid time. In solid times people knew their place in the world, good or bad. Government decisions shaped the lives of their citizens. In liquid times much is unknown and unbounded. Individuals are faced with challenges never previously encountered (Bauman 2006). In these fluid times, cross-national conglomerates, global agencies, media moguls wield increasing influence and power. On many occasions, it is difficult to work out who will sort out an issue, be it a disastrous oil leak or a damaging newspaper leak.

The young people whose accounts we have heard in this book are at the cutting edge of social change. Young people in the cities understand the day-to-day realities of city life. Those in rural South Africa feel the reach of the cities and experience its impact. Bauman captures some of the complexities of city life, identifying the struggles as well as the opportunities:

> . . . nowadays cities are dumping grounds for globally produced troubles: but they may also be seen as laboratories in which the ways and means of living with difference, still to be learned by the residents of an increasingly overcrowded planet, are daily implemented, put to the test, memorised and assimilated . . . Huntington's apocalyptic vision of the irreconcilable conflict and inescapable clash of civilisations can be translated into benign and often deeply gratifying and enjoyable daily encounters with the humanity hiding behind the frighteningly unfamiliar scenic masks of different and mutually alien races, nationalities, gods and liturgies.
>
> (Bauman 2011, p. 92)

These opportunities for 'deeply gratifying and enjoyable encounters' between individuals and groups lie within the reach of schools today. In the contemporary scenario of increasing complexity and fluidity, schools have the opportunity to capture the best of liquid times. This is in the spaces they create for young people to be themselves, and the ways in which they prepare them to be flexible and adaptive and ready to face up to the unknown. For some young people schools can be the spring box to success (Illustration 7.3). For others, school offers them the space to 'be yourself' (Illustration 7.4).

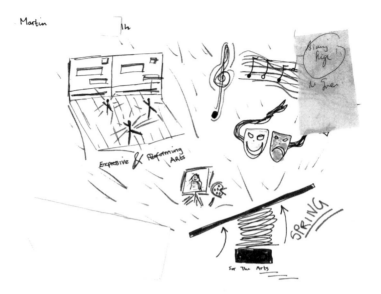

ILLUSTRATION 7.3

ILLUSTRATION 7.4

The archipelago of place and space

When I began the exploratory work for this book my focus was on the senior leaders in a school. However, leaders of place are not only senior leaders, but middle leaders, subject leaders, classroom leaders and young people. Leadership of place is exercised at many levels, from school principals, to young staff such as Kushtrim's tutor, to those young people who work as peer mentors and serve as role models. 'When someone does not have nothing, don't let him cry' says a child from Thandiwe Primary School. The headteacher or principal's job is to nurture that sense of leadership throughout the school.[1]

Within the community, leaders of place come from every walk of life. They can include formal leaders of other institutions and organizations, as well as formal and informal leaders from the area. Leaders from Kagisu Primary and women from the local community came together to set up a cooperative that makes and sells handicrafts. Leadership of place is enriched when all of these disparate leaders come together to seek to make spaces safer, more useful and more meaningful. Leadership of place is about agency. Leaders of place start by identifying the spaces in the school and in the locality which are significant for young people: for their learning, their well-being, their sense of self.

In the introduction to this book, I promised a framework, a roadmap to help leaders become more effective leaders of place. Broadly speaking, this is a theory of action.[2] A theory of action requires:

- *Intent*: a sense of purpose which focuses on supporting young people to find their place in the world

- *Expression*: an articulation of this intent in ways that will enable others to join in

- *Action*: specific plans and activities designed to realize the intent

This is how the theory of action begins. . . .

Imagine young people's lives as being lived in a series of separate spaces. Imagine these spaces as islands within an archipelago. The islands share a common climate but are separated by waters which can sometimes be treacherous. The theory of action is about seeing the big picture in the archipelago. It is about identifying the islands and the spaces between them. It's also about making choices, deciding priorities and figuring out:

- *Which spaces matter most in this archipelago?*

- *How can these spaces be connected?*

Leadership of the archipelago is about making as many connections as possible between the islands. But first it is essential to ask:

- *What's distinctive about this archipelago, this place where I lead?*

Leaders of place build bridges, craft boats, teach the islanders how to swim. They work together with leaders from all of the islands, with the islanders and with young people to reclaim the land. The more bridges and connections that are made between the islands, the more young people will feel free to move around the archipelago, discover new archipelagos and find a place for themselves.

Each archipelago can be very different. For instance, one could be disparate and divided. In the Cobble Hill archipelago, the schools inhabit a very different island from the residents and shopkeepers who live and work close to the school. At the same time, the young people from the Cobble Hill Schools live on islands some distance away.

Some islands can be tightly coupled, such as those of Annie Besant School, where the school's community and the local community are closely linked. Yet, the archipelago they are part of has, in the main, very different characteristics from their own. Archipelagos can change fast. Each school, each island context, is constantly evolving. In Williamsburg, the strong connections between the school and its community are fragmenting and a new archipelago is emerging on the horizon.

The fluidity of the archipelago reconfiguration will shape and reshape young people's lives, their sense of identity, community and place. Thus, leaders of the archipelago need to scan the horizon. They need to look through the lens of their kaleidoscope at the complex, colourful and shifting pattern around them. Having made sense of the changing forms and patterns in their archipelago they need to ask:

- *What actions can I take to be an effective leader of this archipelago, this place?*

Being a leader in this archipelago, this place

One significant part of being a leader in an archipelago is to recognize the importance of school as a place for young people. There are probably three aspects of this:

- *There is the school as a physical environment:* The school is a building, a physical reality. The school environment can be conducive to learning, or it can tax the learner and the teacher.

- *There is the school as an ecology of relationships:* The school can be healthy and caring, or depressing and indifferent, sapping energy. Interpersonal relationships can be balanced or fraught. However, even when the physical conditions are tough – limited water or electricity as in the Eastern Cape – young people can still appreciate the warmth of their teachers, and the important relationships they have there.

- *There is the school as a narrative:* The experience of school life contributes to a young person's emotional map, their sense of self and their sense of their place in the world.

Each of these three notions of place generates its own questions for school leaders to think about from their own experience and that of the young people in their care:

- *The physical environment:* How do you feel when you cross the threshold of the school?

- *The ecology of relationships:* How do others respond to you, behave towards you?

- *The narrative:* What messages does the school give you about yourself? Are you acknowledged? Welcomed?

Schools are places that matter. They can open doors for young people. And close them too. An essential part of leadership of place, leadership within the archipelago, is to create spaces for young people, both in the school and the locality. Space is where identity is enacted, where values are instilled or challenged. These values can be democratic or hierarchical. Creating these spaces has an impact on young people – their confidence, their sense of self – and on their families. Mothers of the young women at Annie Besant step into a learning space in the school and by so doing also step into the world.

There are the spaces to be fashioned within the school and throughout the wider archipelago. Once these spaces are formed, the links and connections made between the islands, the archipelago becomes a rich and fulfilling place to inhabit.

Creating the spaces within the school

There are three particular types of spaces within the school that are particularly meaningful to young people in enabling them to explore their identity:

Space 1: An inhabited space which is safe and inspirational

Space 2: A space for different cultures and values to be accepted

Space 3: A space for young people to speak out about what troubles them and what is important to them

Space 1: *An Inhabited space which is safe and inspirational*

The place we inhabit shapes our expectations and our aspirations. Inhabited space influences how people see their place in society (Ramphele 1993). It provides individuals with cues that encourage them to expand or contract their expectations. For young people, the inhabited space in the school needs to be a safe one: free from the power of bullies, the reach of gangs.

The speed of change in our liquid times reinforces the importance of the inhabited space in the school. In Chapter 3, Rachel, a London headteacher, described the rapidity of change in the composition of her school. The school's population had shifted from being predominantly white working-class to being ethnically diverse. The pattern of diversity continued to evolve: the Vietnamese immigrant community of the past replaced by Somalians, Nigerians and Nepalese.

For Rachel, leadership of place was about 'creating physical conditions that match the aspirations for young people in terms of relationships, experiences and educational outcomes'. Leadership of place had to start with what children brought with them. It had to progress to ensuring that they knew who they were in British society:

> Young people bring with them an experience of a place and community which can be dangerous. My thinking has changed as time has gone on. I've been very aware of the high level of mobility in this locality and that the only way that you can create stability is in this place, the school.
>
> The art of leadership of place is how you enable those young people who come to live in Britain, to be who they are in British society. This is about helping them enjoy their own personal cultural experiences and history and know their own story.

Leadership of place was also about ensuring that the school's environment took into account the physical conditions young people encountered in their daily lives. The school needed to provide the space for children to breathe and feel safe:

> Leaders need to look at the relationship of users to the place. For example, is there graffiti or litter? Do children feel they have a vested interest? Do they refuse to use the toilets because they're worried? Do they go past smokers? Is this an easy conformable place where children feel enabled? Are the classrooms fit for purpose? What about the materials? The environment?
>
> We use primary colours in corridors to embolden and enliven. These are not the muted tones of institutions. We go for warmth and brightness. Cushioned Flooring. Good acoustics.

Space 2: *A space for different cultures and values to be understood*

The importance of creating the spaces for different cultures to be valued and understood has particular immediacy in ethnically diverse schools that regularly receive students who are refugees or asylum seekers. The Reach Community School in London is one of these. It has adopted explicit policies and practices to manage the transition of these young people into the life of the school. The principal, Mary, explained the school's approach in the following terms:

> Understanding diversity is the starting point. You cannot operate in a school like this if you have fixed ideas of how other people think. Understanding diversity is the first step towards establishing mutual respect and dealing with behaviour. It also conditions how we teach our pupils who often are bilingual, but have language and literacy skills well below the national average.

There is a refugee co-ordinator who produces a bulletin for staff about the newcomers to the school to ensure that staff understand the lives of the young people as they arrive. There are regular briefing sessions. The principal sees part of her role as managing competing realities. 'I saw a member of staff upset about a dress code misdemeanour', she said, 'I reminded her that that child had seen her mother being murdered'. Meeting with a group of staff to discuss the challenges of working in such a diverse school, they told me about the importance of expectations and beliefs. They emphasized boosting and maintaining the self-esteem of pupils. This was a very fragile commodity.

This conversation took me back to Kushtrim. In response to his exclusion from the school, his tutor had drawn up an alternative scenario. This scenario mirrored the thinking and practice of staff at the Reach, beginning with the kind of staff briefing that the Reach held regularly:

> A training session was conducted . . . and teachers learned about the circumstances regarding Kushtrim's reasons for coming to the UK . . . They were asked to anticipate the difficulties he was likely to have in the school given his difficult history and cultural differences . . . , They devised 'coping' strategies and agreed to revise them half-termly. . . .
> (They) learned that linguistic and communicative competence were quite distinct and not to be confused. They agreed to avoid confrontation and arguments with Kushtrim until he developed

sufficient communicative competence and brainstormed ways of ensuring that Kushtrim complied with the school rules without conflict. . . .

What appeared to be the biggest challenge for Kustrim was adopting more culturally appropriate ways of communicating with people, especially adults in power. His tutor explained to him that raising his voice would provoke a dismissive reaction in the UK, while threatening behaviour . . . would be taken very seriously . . . She told him, "Why don't you put your Albanian eagle closer to your heart – under your shirt?" The deputy took upon himself to have regular communication with Kushtrim's guardian and social services to ensure that he was supported on all fronts.

The school managed to build a trustful relationship with Kushtrim. He took 7 GCSEs and went to college to become an electrician. One day . . . he drove to Tirana in his Mercedes smiling at the thought of how proud his parents would be with him when they finally saw him.

(Adapted from Stabler 2011)

This ideal scenario requires resources. Nonetheless, the time taken to prevent cultural misunderstandings with the 'Kushtrims' in our school systems is probably considerably less than that taken to resolve them. The impact on their self-esteem, their identity, and their ability to make the transition to a new place is incalculable.

Paying attention to the emotional dissonance felt by young people who are 'outsiders' is only part of the challenge of leadership of place. A different set of challenges emerges when established communities feel they are being pushed out; whether they are the white working-class communities of London or the Hispanic communities of Brooklyn. The reactions and alienation of those who have been the insiders but who feel they are becoming the outsiders have to be dealt with.

Space 3: *A space for young people to speak out about what troubles them and what is important to them*

Young people will only speak out if they experience school as a safe place and one that engages with them and their lives. Bob from Cobble Hill described this in the following terms:

I just want to create a place that kids can feel safe to be who they are. That's a learning environment of rapport, respect, competence, and love. Kids can smell it. They know when it is there and when it's not.

At Annie Besant, this notion of safety was paramount. It was the prerequisite to creating a 'constructive environment' where students could talk about cultural issues and express their concerns, for example, about racism. The spaces for discussion included a Political Forum to talk about controversial issues. At Mere School, Hackney, its diverse community members, many of whom were new arrivals in the country, were offered a supportive space to talk about common problems. As a leader in that archipelago, Anna saw an important part of her role as 'joining up the dots', making broader connections and 'enriching the soil'.

Creating the spaces within the wider archipelago

There are three further aspects of space that reach more directly out into the archipelago.

Space 4: A space to challenge the lure of the streets and reclaim them

Space 5: A space to build trust and develop social capital

Space 6: A space to embrace and celebrate diversity

Space 4: *A space to challenge the lure of the streets and reclaim them*

The Rights of Passage Programme at Downtown School in Brooklyn brought adults from the community into the school to work with students. This included gang leaders who had street credibility. The programme recognized the attractions of street-life and gave young people the opportunity to discuss highly contentious issues in a safe environment. Sadly, the school lost funding for this programme.

The programme of active engagement with community to challenge the lure of the streets was also strong at Themba High

School in the Eastern Cape. The school brought in community members to present an alternative reality. As Tau put it, they work to show their learners that 'stealing from others is only a temporary way out of poverty. But it's hard for the child who goes home hungry'. The unequivocal message was 'going to jail is a bad start'.

Space 5: *A space to build trust and develop social capital*

An archipelago will function best when there is trust between the islands and islanders and when the talents of all are recognized. Throughout this book's pages, there have been many examples of the ways that school leaders have placed trust centre stage in what they did. They have typically emphasized the importance of not pre-judging people, of starting from a position of inclusion, of developing trust by building bridges and strengthening connections. The lure of the street is challenged when there is a strong bond of trust between the young people, school staff, families and communities. When trust is in the ether, the archipelago becomes a much healthier place to live in.

However, this book has also shown a second reality. There are times, as Carla at Downtown demonstrated so vividly, where building trust with families does not work. There are times when the school's job is to inoculate its young people against the potential harm in their lives or communities, to build up their immune systems. And for some young people there are times when they have to break the link with their families and communities in order to be free to be who they are and find their place in the world. The lesson for the school leader of the archipelago is that there are some islands they cannot change.

Building trust requires energy, commitment and focus. However, the importance of building trust cannot be underestimated (Byrk and Schneider 2002; Louis 2007). Trust is a dynamic concept, an essential ingredient for building an archipelago which is based on cooperative action. Trust is also the foundation of social capital (Coleman 1988, 1990). It enables us to recognize the 'invisible assets', the untapped resources of communities (Hargreaves 2003), such as the handicraft skills of the women in the Eastern Cape. Young people have an important role to play in developing trust between their school and the local community.

Space 6: *A space to embrace and celebrate diversity*

All too often the diversity of many of our city schools is presented as a problem, rather than an opportunity. Yet in 2012 the New York Times reported that a growing number of foreign-born affluent New Yorkers, especially those from Western Europe, were now sending their children to public schools. In a city where the affluent tend to educate their children in private schools, this is an interesting trend. These 'new' New Yorkers are attracted by the ethnic and economic diversity of public schools. They believe that sending their children to schools which are diverse will help them to understand and value different cultures and become part of the wider American community (Temple 2012).

Throughout this book, there are many examples of the positive benefits of knowing someone who is 'not like me'. Children who are in schools which are diverse welcome that diversity. Where different groups of people are neighbours, it reduces conflict and misunderstanding. A recent UK survey found that despite Britain becoming a more diverse society, nearly half of white Britons only interact with a person from a different ethnic background when being served in a restaurant or shop (Guardian 2012; ONS 2011, 2012).

Diversity is an increasing reality. The response to meeting 'someone different from me' can be 'How interesting!' Or ... 'How scary!' The growing diversity in society today presents school leaders with many challenges and richness of opportunities. For leaders in their archipelagos there are many questions about the fusion of ideas and practice, such as:

- What attitudes do you work to induce?

- How do you create understanding between communities which live separate lives?

A Place where I belong

Our sense of belonging is shaped by our views about who we are, what our tribe is, who we would like to be and what we experience along the way. Leadership of place is about making sense of the complexity and significance of these issues for young people. It is about making sense of the movements and patterns in their lives, what they think and experience within their neighbourhood, where they feel safe, where they and their families feel they belong. It is about making sense of the many ways in which the political landscape shapes young people's lives and experiences – and the potential for conflict within localities in which ideas, beliefs, aspirations and values are contested and opposing forces fight for their space. And it is about making sense of, and recreating, what they experience when they cross the threshold into school. Each archipelago has its own pattern, its own story to tell.

In our increasingly fluid world, we need to understand why the city is as it is and what young people can do to change it. What can they do to shape and reshape the archipelagos in which they spend their lives and to create new archipelagos? In many countries, levels of political literacy are low. Here I draw from Paulo Freire's rich reflections on the challenges of urban education. Freire argued that schools need to be able to make the connections between conventional forms of literacy and between informed democratic political consciousnesses. 'Literacy', he argued, 'involves not just the reading of the word, but the reading of the world' (Freire 1993, p. 59). Freire wanted to encourage the practice of critical enquiry in young people: that notion of constantly asking questions about what the world is and how their community, their country, their city, their world is shaped by structural inequalities, political decisions, gender, race, disability, class (Grace 2010).

Leadership of place and the development of political literacy are connected by the potential for schools to play a pivotal role in creating a 'buy in' for young people. This buy in will enable them to make sense of the place in which they are located, and recognize how they can influence and shape it (Riley 2012). Once they have been given the spaces in their archipelagos to be themselves, they will begin to think, I have had this space for me. I have found a place for me. Now what can I do to give back to this community, this archipelago? Other archipelagos?

To be able to think and contribute as a global citizen, young people first need to be secure in *who* they are and *where* they come from. They have to be able to think local before they can think global. Having a sense of place and location – and a view that they can influence their own lives – will free them to take up their role as a global citizen. Our hopes, dreams and aspirations for our children and young people need to be boundless . . .

Questions for discussion and reflection

1 The chapter suggests that there are three notions of place: the physical environment: the ecology of relationships and the narrative. Think about each of these and answer the questions below:

- *The physical environment:* How do you feel when you cross the threshold of the school?
- *The ecology of relationships:* How do others respond to you, behave towards you?
- What messages does the school give you about yourself? Are you acknowledged? Welcomed?

2 Now put yourself in the shoes of the young people on your school and answer the three questions again.

3 The archipelago of place and space:

- What's distinctive about the archipelago, the place where you lead?
- Which spaces matter most in this archipelago? (inside the school and outside)
- How can these spaces be connected?

Notes

1   Elsewhere I have provided examples of reflective and analytical tools that will help schools to audit and map the community context and gain greater understanding of the needs of young people and communities (Riley 2008a).

2   Elsewhere I have put forward the idea of a theory of action for strengthening the relationships between schools and communities. That model has three parts: Bridging, Challenging and Building (Riley 2012).

REFERENCES

Anderson, G. (2009) *Advocacy Leadership: Toward a Post-Reform Agenda*, New York: Routledge.

Bauch, P. (2001) School-community partnerships in rural schools: renewal and a sense of place, *Peabody Journal of Education*, 76 (2), 204–21.

Bauman, Z. (2006) *Liquid Times: Living in an Age of Uncertainty*, Cambridge: Polity.

—(2011) The London Riots – on consumerism coming home to roost, *Social Europe Journal*, 9th September, www.social-europe

BBC (2004) Porter pays £12m to Westminster, 5th July, www.news. bbc.c.uk/2/hi/386787.stm

—(2009) Free school meals, http://news.bbc.co.uk/1/hi/education/8194464.stm, 11 August 2009, accessed 13th February 2012.

—(2010) Boris Johnson won't accept 'Kosovo-style' social cleansing, 28th October, www.bbc.co.uk/-politics-11643440.

Bennington, J. and Hartley, J. (2009) *Whole Systems Go!: Improving Leadership across the Whole Public System*, Report by The Sunningdale Institute, National School of Government.

Berg, A. C., Melaville, A. and Blank, M. J. (2006) *Community and Family Engagement: Principals Share What Works*, Washington: Coalition for Community Schools.

Bernstein, B. (1977) *Class, Codes and Control, Vol. 3*, London: Routledge & Kegan Paul.

Blackhurst, C. (1995) Tory group 'risked lives of tenants', *The Independent*, London: 30 November, p. 7.

Block, D. (2006) *Multilingual Identities in a Global City: London stories*, Basingstoke: Palgrave.

Boltwood, S. (2007) *Brian Friel, Ireland, and The North*, Cambridge: Cambridge University Press.

Bourdieu, P. (1999) Site effects, in P. Bourdieu et al. (eds), *The Weight of the World: Social Suffering in Contemporary Society* (P. P. Ferguson, Trans), Stanford: Stanford University Press.

Byrk, A. and Schneider, B. (2002) *Trust in Schools: A Core Resource for Improvement*, New York: Russell Sage Foundation.

Cantle Report (2001) *Community Cohesion: A Report of the Independent Review Team*, London: Home Office.

Cohen, R. (1997) *Global Diasporas: An Introduction*, London: UCL Press.

Coleman, J. (1988) Social capital in the creation of human capital, *American Journal of Sociology, 94*, 95–120.

— (1990) *Foundations of Social Theory*, USA: Harvard University Press.

Collinge, J., Gibney, J. and Mabey, C. (2010) (eds) *Leadership and Place*, London: Routledge.

Copsey, N. (2004) *Contemporary British Fascism: The British National Party and the Quest for Legitimacy*, Basingstoke: Palgrave Macmillan.

Cresswell, T. (2004) *Place: A Short Introduction*, Oxford and MA: Blackwell.

Department for Children and Family Services (2007) *Guidance on the Duty to Promote Community Cohesion*, London: DCFS.

Dillabough, J. and Kenelly, J. (2009) Lost Youth in the Global City Class, Culture and the Urban Imaginary, London: Taylor and Francis.

Dillabough, J-A. and Kennelly, J. (2010) *Lost Youth in the Global City: Class Culture and the Urban Imagery*, London: Routledge.

Dyson, A. and Gallannaugh, F. (2008) *School-level actions to promote community cohesion: a scoping map*. Technical report, in: Research Evidence in Education Library, London: EPPI-Centre, Social Science Research Unit, Institute of Education, University of London.

Eade, J. (2000) *Placing London: From Imperial Capital to Global City*, London: Berghahn Books.

Forrest, R. and Kearns, A. (2001) Social cohesion, social capital and the neighbourhood, *Urban Studies, 38* (12), 2125–43.

Freire, P. (1993) Challenges of urban education, in P. Freire (ed.) *Pedagogy of the City*, New York: Continuum.

Fried, A. and Elman, R. (eds) (1968) *Charles Booth's London*, London: Pantheon books.

Gans, H. J. (1962) *The Urban Villagers: Group and Class in the Life of Italian-Americans*, New York: Free Press of Glencoe.

Gibney, J., Yapps, C., Trickett, S. and Collinge, C. (2009) *The New 'place' Shaping: The Implications for Leaders in Further Education*, Birmingham: Centre for Urban and Regional Studies, Birmingham Business School, University of Birmingham.

Grace, G. (1978) *Teachers, Ideology and Control: A Study in Urban Education*, London: Routledge and Kegan Paul.

— (2006) Urban education: confronting the contradictions: an analysis with special reference to London, *London Review of Education, 4* (2), 115–31.

— (2010) Political Literacy: A Response to K. A. Riley (2010) *Are London's Schools Meeting the Needs of Today's Young People?* Professorial Lecture, London: Institute of Education.

Guardian (2001) Guardian Unlimited, 12 December 2001, URL accessed 19 June 2006.

— (2008) http://www.guardian.co.uk/uk/2008/dec/11/counter-terrorism-strategy-extremists (Alan Travis).

— (2009) http://www.guardian.co.uk/uk/2009/oct/18/prevent-extremism-muslims-information-allegations (Vikram Dodd).

— (2011) Cameron's crackdown underway as cash withheld from 'suspect' groups: Patrick Wintour & Jenny Percival, 7th February, p. 4.

— (2012) How do you mix with other ethnicities? 28th February, p. 10.

Hague, C. and Jenkins, P. (2005) *Place Identity, Planning and Participation*, London and New York: Routledge.

Hannerz, U. (1996) *Transnational Connections: Culture, People, Places*, London: Routledge.

Hargreaves, A. (2003) *Leadership for transformation within the London Challenge*, Annual Lecture of the London Leadership Centre, Institute of Education, May.

Higham, R. (2010) Young people's experiences and perceptions of ethnic diversity and community cohesion in London: a review. Working Paper, London Education Research Unit, London: Institute of Education.

Home Office (2006) *Report into the Terrorist Attacks, 7th July 2005*, London: HMSO.

Ipsos Mori (2008) Understanding Social Capital in Camden: Findings from the 2008 Social Capital Survey.

Kahin, M. (1997) *Education Somali Children in Britain*, Staffordshire: Trentham Books.

Kearney, A. T. (2008) *The Chicago Council on Global Affairs, and Washington Post*, Newsweek Interactive, LLC.

Logan, D., King, J., and Fischer-Wright, H. (2008) *Tribal Leadership, Leveraging Natural Groups to Build a Thriving Organization*, New York: Harper Collins Publishing.

London, J. (1903) *The people of the Abyss*, London: MacMillan.

Long, R. E. (2003) 'West Side Story' *Broadway, The Golden Years: Jerome Robbins and The Great Choreographer-Directors: 1940 to the present*, Continuum International Publishing Group.

Louis, K. S. (2007) Trust and improvement in schools, *Journal of Educational Change*, 8 (1), 1–25.

MacBeath, J. and Dempster, N. (eds) (2009) *Connecting Leadership and Learning: Principles for Practice*, New York and London: Routledge.

MacBeath, J., Moos, L. and Riley, K. A. (1996) Leadership in a changing world, in K. Leithwood, K. Chapman, C. Corson, P. Hallinger and A. Hart (eds) *International Handbook for Educational Leadership and Administration*, The Netherlands: Kluwer Academic Publishers.

Magill (2001) Magill v. Weeks, UKHL 67 (13th December).

McRobbie, A. (1991) *Feminism and Youth Culture*, London: Unwin Hyman.

Megan Meier Foundation (2011) www.meganmeierfoundation.org/ mission statement, accessed February 2012.

Mehmedbegovic, D. (2007) 'Miss who needs the languages of immigrants' London's Multilingual School, in T. Brighouse and L. Fullick (eds), *Education in a Global City: Essays from London*, London: Institute of Education.

Murphy, J. and Louis, K. S. (1994) *Reshaping the Principalship: Insights for Transformational Efforts*, Thousand Islands California, CA: Corwin Press.

Nastasi, J. and Porath, J. (2010) *The City Repair Project: Transforming Space into Place*, (DVD) Portland, OR: Luana Films.

New York Times (2011) 7th September, Diary, p. 7.

Ogbu, J. (1992) Understanding cultural diversity and learning, *Educational Researcher, 21*, 5–14.

Ogbu, J. U. and Simons, H. D. (1998) Voluntary and involuntary minorities: a cultural-ecological theory of school performance with some implications for education, *Anthropology and Education Quarterly, 29*, 155–88.

ONS (2007) *Mid-2007 Population Estimates: Ethnicity* (Tables_EE1_ EE6).xls, London: Office for National Statistics.

—(2011) *Measuring Children and Young People's Well Being*, London: Office for National Statistics & Cardiff: BRASS, University of Cardiff, Supplementary Paper.

—(2012) *Measuring Children and Young People's Well Being: Our Relationships*, London: Office for National Statistics, 28th February.

Palmer, A. (1989) *The East End*, London: Alan Palmer.

Poverty Profile (2009) London Poverty Profile, available at: www. londonspovertyprofile.org.uk/about/overall-key-findings/, www. londonspovertyprofile.org.uk/indicators/topics/income-poverty/ childpoverty and www.londonspovertyprofile.org.uk/Indicators/topics/ income-poverty/poverty-in-inner-and-outer-london. Also reported in http://www.guardian.co.uk/politics/2009/may/19/london-poverty

Putnam, R. D. (2007) E pluribus unum: diversity and community in the twenty-first century, the 2006 Johan Skytte prize lecture, *Scandinavian Political Studies, 30* (2), 137–74.

Ramphele, M. (1993) *A Bed Called Home: Life in the Migrant Labour Hostels of Cape Town*, Cape town: David Phillip.

—(2008) *Laying Ghosts to Rest: Dilemmas of the Transformation in South Africa*, Cape Town: Tafelberg Publisher.

Ranson, S. and Crouch, C. (2009) *Towards a New Governance of Schools in the Remaking of Civil Society*, Reading: CfBT Education Trust.

Rasmussen, J. (2009) Education for Somali students in London: challenges and strategies, *Malcaster Abroad: Research and Writing from Off-Campus Study*: Vol. 3, 1, 4. http://digitalcommons.macalester.edu/

Ravitch, D. (2010) *The Death and Life of the Great American School System: How Testing and Choice are Undermining Education*, New York: Basic Books.

Riley, K. A. (1998) *Whose School is it Anyway?* London: Falmer Press, New York: Taylor and Francis.

—(2008a) *Surviving and Thriving as an Urban Leader: Reflective and Analytical Tools for Leaders of Our City Schools*, London: Esme Fairburn Foundation, Institute of Education.

—(2008b) Improving city schools: who and what makes the difference? in C. Sugrue (ed.) *New Directions for Educational Change: International Perspectives*, London: Routledge.

—(2010) *Are London's Schools Meeting the Needs of Today's Young People?* Professorial Lecture, London: Institute of Education.

—(2012) Forthcoming, walking the leadership tight-rope: building community cohesiveness & social capital in schools in highly disadvantaged urban communities, *British Educational Research Journal*.

Riley, K. A. and Louis, K. S. (2000) *Leadership for Change and School Reform: International Perspectives*, London and New York: Routledge.

Riley, K. A. and Stoll, L. (2005) *Leading Communities: Purposes, Paradoxes and Possibilities*, Professorial Lecture, London: Institute of Education.

Riley, K. and West-Burnam, J. (2003) *Educational Leadership in London*, Discussion Document, Nottingham: National College for School Leadership.

— (2004) *The Challenges of Leadership in London*, Nottingham: National College for School Leadership.

Riley, K., Hesketh, T., Rafferty, S., Taylor-Moore, P., Young, J. and Beecham, Y. (2005) *Urban Pioneers – Leading the Way Ahead: First Lessons from the Leadership on the Front-line Project*, London: Institute of Education, University of London, Issues in Practice Series.

Sassen, S. (1991) *The Global City: New York, London, Tokyo*, Princeton: University Press.

— (2001) *The Global City: New York, London, Tokyo*, US: Princetown University Press.

Sheridan, Y. (2001) *Germany Calling – Lord Haw-Haw, Collaborator and Broadcaster From Here to Obscurity*, London: Tenterbooks.

Shukra, K., Back, L., Keith, M., Khan, A. and Solomos, J. (2004) Race, social cohesion and the changing politics of citizenship, *London Review of Education*, 2 (3), 187–98.

Stabler, V. (2011) 'Involuntary' minority students: how to get excluded from an all-inclusive school, Assignment, MA in Leadership, *Leading in Diverse Cultures and Communities*, London: Institute of Education.

Stern, S. (2011) Lots of children left behind, *City Journal*, 9th December. http://www.city-journal.org/2011/eon1209ss.html

Strauss, V. (2010) A student play blasting N.Y. school reform is banned, *The Washington Post*, 23rd December, http://voices.washingtonpost. com/answer-sheet/school-turnaroundsreform/a-student-play-criticizing-sch.html

— (2011) Joel Klein's snow job, The Answer Sheet Archive: Marc Epstein, *The Washington Post*, 11th January 2011, http://voices. washingtonpost.com/answer-sheet/marc-epstein/

Temple, K. (2012) *New York Times*, Observer, 26th February 2012, p. 7.

Tunstall, R., Lupton, R., Kneale, D. and Jenkins, A. (2011) Growing up in social housing in the new millennium: housing, neighbourhoods, and early outcomes for children born in 2000, London: CASE & London School of Economics, CASE/143.

Un-Habitat (2005) World Habitat Day 2005, http://www.unhabitat.org/

Urban Adventures (2012) www.urbanadventures.com/london_tour_east_london_uncovered, accessed 13th February 2012.

Usmayors.org (2012) 20th January. www.usmayors.org/80thWinterMeeting/

Vincent, K. (2011) 'Liminal learners' in a global city: the education of Bangladeshi girls in an east London secondary school. Institutional Focused Study: Institute of Education University of London, September.

Waltham Forest (2007) *Young Voice Survey White and Asian youths*, London: London Borough of Waltham Forest.

Wikipedia (2012) http://en.wikipedia.org/wiki/Brian_Friel, accessed 17th March.

Willis, P. (1977) *Learning to Labour*, London: Ashgate.

Young, M. and Wilmott, P. (1957) *Family and Kinship in East London*, London: Routledge and Kegan Paul.

INDEX